THE ONLY FREEDOM

Books by BARRY WOOD

The Magnificent Frolic
The Only Freedom

THE
ONLY
FREEDOM

by BARRY WOOD

THE WESTMINSTER PRESS
Philadelphia

Library of Congress Cataloging in Publication Data

Wood, Barry, 1940–
   The only freedom.

   Includes bibliographical references.
   1. Liberty. I. Title.
HM271.W65   128'.3   71–190361
ISBN 0–664–20940–8

For My Wife,
SHARI,

*A free person
who believes in
only a few things,
and doesn't take
even these
too seriously*

Contents

Contents

Foreword

FOR SOME TIME NOW I have been fascinated by those people who claim to have discovered true freedom through one or another religion, political philosophy, or revolutionary ideology. When such liberated people are challenged or closely questioned they usually become defensive and angry, as if their freedom would somehow "escape" unless protected by the intellectual equivalent of armored defense.

This book examines the idea that these conceptual certainties do not bring freedom but enslavement, since the one thing these "free" people are not free to do is to abandon their conceptual systems. It is written out of the profound conviction that mental health and human survival are possible only for men liberated from psychological chains of their own making. It contends that all efforts to liberate ourselves are enslaving, since the freedom attained through effort is a purely conceptual freedom and the self that approaches life as a task is an abstract self.

Individually and collectively we have a choice to make. We can shipwreck a whole civilization on the ideology of power, progress, and technique. We can enslave ourselves to ideas, abstractions, and symbols. We can destroy ourselves through fanatical devotion to our own worst selves.

Or—without waiting for a "revolution," without the dawn of a "new age"—we can be free.

This is admittedly difficult to grasp for a people who believe that freedom is the *result* of progress, the *purpose* of power, and the *possession* of the individual—or a radical minority who believe it to be the goal of revolution. But as long as these myths prevail, freedom itself will remain unrealized. It is only through the shedding of all such abstract, symbolic, or conceptual freedoms that the way is open for the experience itself of being truly free.

I should warn the reader—whether he be an arch conservative or a militant revolutionary—that he will be annoyed by much in this book. He will find, whatever his own views, a host of inflammatory remarks, including the dismissal of entire systems of thought, points of view, and intellectual positions that he may deem sacred. The point is, however, that if writers simply mouth conventional wisdom, adding a stamp of approval to ideas the reader already accepts, they fail to perform any social function that is not already performed by most television programming. There ought to be a few philosophers around who mainly stir up trouble if only to keep the social sediment from packing down too firmly.

To a certain extent, the turmoil that the reader feels is intentional on my part. It is the purpose of this book to expose wherever possible the flimsy fabric of most of our habitual assumptions. This is easily mistaken for anarchy or sensationalism, though I assure the reader that neither are here intended. What is intended is the communication of a radical freedom quite unlike those versions we have become accustomed to. Its very nature is bound to be unsettling.

More and more, it seems, modern civilization is becoming a House of Cards based upon very shaky ideas about

ourselves, our world, and the meaning of our collective
lives. Many people have suspected this for some time, and
are therefore caught in a traumatic dilemma of what to do
about it. Attempting to preserve the House not only reinforces these flimsy ideas but also ensures that the
destruction will be immense when at last the roof comes
tumbling down around us—as I suspect it may. But the
suggestion that we can and perhaps should live without this
House is equally disturbing, since it leaves us feeling completely exposed—without a roof over our heads, so to
speak.

The fact is that we *do* rely on our ideas as much as we
rely on our houses. The freedom advocated in this book will
therefore seem to some like the intellectual equivalent of
living without any roofs whatever. But in the same way that
roofs require constant repairing, so do concepts, creeds,
ideologies, and abstractions—which become in time the
rickety beams of the mind. Eventually they become brittle
and constricting, requiring continual propping and bracing
if they are to stand at all. The time comes when such a roof
is no protection at all, and we are better off in the open air.

All of this is to say that outmoded ideas, ideologies, and
intellectual systems can be more dangerous than beneficial.
It is a truism that reason is the distinctive characteristic of
man, and the implication generally is that reason is man's
ultimate salvation. What is rarely noted are the dangers and
excesses all too common even among the most "reasonable"
men. In our own time it has become apparent that intellectual solutions often simply aggravate problems, and that
reason alone seems quite unable to cope with the hurricane
of political, social, military, and ecological problems now
besetting mankind.

The more important issue here, however, is one that

ranges into the areas of psychological and emotional health, verging into what might usefully be called relational therapy. I regard freedom from conceptual systems as one side of the coin, the reverse of which involves a real reconciliation with the rest of life—with the more volatile aspects of our own unconscious feelings, with the vulnerability of the body to pain as well as to pleasure, and with the experience of death itself. For along with a fanatical enslavement to purely conceptual values has gone the denigration of the whole instinctual, emotional, and physical side of life. Tied to concepts, we have even tried to deal with this deeper side of life conceptually—with almost no success and sometimes disastrous results. The point is, however, that the recovery of the physical, emotional, and instinctual side of life is crucial to that mode of relational feeling at the heart of wholeness, personal integration, and freedom.

It is only fair to note that I regard a great deal of what is discussed in this book as still open to question. This is necessarily the case whenever one ventures into the quicksand areas of primitive mentality, the origins of urban culture, the psychology of religion, the nature of the unconscious, what happens in perception, or the reasons for our increasing plethora of psychological disturbances. Or, for that matter, the ultimate results of overreliance on technology and overconsumption of natural resources. While we would all like some answers, no one can presume to have the "inside dope" on any of these issues, let alone all of them. My approach has been to describe our present situation as I see it, and to avoid prophecy, of which we have all had enough.

The reader should perhaps remind himself of this if I appear to be "forcing" the evidence. While the book-buying public demands a semblance of consistency and the impression of getting The Truth from someone who *knows*, I do not possess some "monotheory" to explain everything and to chart the future. I leave that up to the monthly magazines in the supermarkets. I have deliberately avoided any approach that requires "consistency at all costs," and I expect that the attentive reader can compile a list of problems not dealt with. I am not disturbed by this. To wait until absolutely everything falls into place, to demand a watertight proof for every statement, is to ensure that nothing will be said. Moreover, "consistency" and "certainty" are some of those enslaving demands put upon philosophers in a universe that is full of loose ends and runny edges.

Those who have read my former book, *The Magnificent Frolic,* will recognize a similarity, the present work being an expansion and refinement of its final chapter. Freedom from creeds, codes, and cults in that earlier work has here been extended to include freedom from absolutes and abstractions of all kinds: political, philosophical, social, psychological. This is intended neither as a manifesto for nihilism nor as a return to primitivism, but as a challenge to liberate ourselves from, in the sense of "seeing through," most of the claptrap in our heads.

The reader may call this anything he likes: self-therapy, applied Zen, Buddhist metaphysics, intellectual yoga. I have preferred to leave it free of tags in the belief that any name for freedom may prejudice the mind and block freedom itself. The reader who feels that I am hedging or refusing to adopt a final position has gotten *the* point. Anyone who expects a neat formula or program for attaining freedom might well stick to the monthly magazines, already mentioned. Finally, everything I have said about ideas must also be applied to the ideas in this book. Any attachment to my ideas, as to any others, can only sabotage freedom. Inasmuch as any writer enjoys devoted readers, I am pleased for those who respond to what I have to say. But my advice must be to read this book only if you must, and if you do— forget it as quickly as possible.

I now realize that the beginnings of this book date back to well before the first outline was set on paper early in the spring of 1971. Virtually all of my thinking life I have had doubts about most of the things I was told, whether philosophical, religious, political, or moral. I am certain about very few things. Almost nothing I have read has convinced me that civilized man knows what he is up to.

To this primary feeling has been added the experience of ten years on three university campuses. These years have convinced me that the highest intellects in the land are far too certain about most of their ideas—but uncertain as to why. Two years in the midst of this were spent teaching high school, during which time the curriculum required me to teach ideas based on many untested and uncertain assumptions. The result was the rather humbling experience of having participated in the mental enslavement of about two hundred fifty teen-agers.

For a brief period quite recently I believed that a real liberation of the mind was occurring in America, as young people everywhere opposed military service, challenged established values, and began developing their own counter-culture. There were signs in high places, too, of a vast dissatisfaction with the manipulation of the public by both the government and the advertisers. A whole new thought-style seemed to be emerging, and new life-styles were being explored not only on the campus but in enclaves both urban and rural all across the country. Over the years I had watched many of my friends growing, emerging, firming up new value systems for themselves which had nothing to do with capitalism, rugged individualism, consumerism, or any of the other accepted trends of modern American life. For me, all of this reached a kind of culmination with the publication of Charles Reich's *The Greening of America* late in 1970, a book that seemed to crystallize my own half-articulate feelings.

What forced me to rethink all this was a seminar that I taught at the request of some students at Stanford University in the winter quarter of 1971. Ostensibly, this seminar carried the title "Varieties of Religious Experience." It evolved, however, into a sweeping look at the fundamental assumptions of civilized man, and might well be retitled "Ways of Looking at It." By the end of the quarter I no longer believed that any recognizable group possessed the key to the problems of American society—a conclusion that for me grew out of the whole context of that seminar.

Winter, 1971, was a bad quarter for Stanford University. There was a great deal of violent and destructive activism on and near the campus, including many thousands of dollars of property damage and personal loss. Some of the more familiar events have had a protracted history in the national press, culminating in the January, 1972, firing of a tenured professor of English with Maoist persuasions, Bruce Franklin. During the quarter some of my own students were marginally involved in the "trashing" of university buildings, and many had elaborate justifications for their actions. The pressures of these events forced us into considerable discussion around the problem of human freedom from almost every point of view. Perhaps because I neither condoned nor condemned these actions, some semblance of communication continued on the issues at hand.

At the end of this seminar I was convinced that many of these students were severely restricted by their own ideas: by rigorous expectations about how the university *should* be run, how America *ought* to be governed and by whom, the *best* way to end the war, and the *correct* course of action for achieving human dignity and freedom. I soon came to feel that this very enslavement to ideas was itself the central issue for the problem of human freedom. It seemed clear, for example, that underneath most of the raging controversies of our time, beneath most of our conflicting beliefs and ideologies, are a few shared assumptions to which almost everyone is blind. Because of this blindness, human problem-solving quite regularly turns into knot-tying, with very little penetration to the nature of our dilemma. Just about any problem in the areas of ecology, racism, urban renewal, crime control, disarmament, or international peacekeeping would serve to illustrate the kind of knots to which I refer. I concluded that since the whole of Western civilization is literally tangled in its own bad assumptions, freedom must begin with some radical surgery to be performed on our cultural assumptions.

Out of these reflections the following book has grown. The stimulus for its writing was an immediate situation, but the issues span centuries. In a sense the freedom here developed is of immense antiquity, since it traces in one form or another to the "liberation" of Mahayana Buddhism, Hinduism, and Japanese Zen. But instead of writing a book on Oriental philosophy, of which there are many, I have preferred to let the ideas stand on their own, with only an occasional reference to these ancient sources. The reader who finds the approach of this book an appealing one is advised to go directly to these sources, where he will find a precedent for almost everything I have said.

Special thanks are due to those members of Zeta Alpha Pi (ZAP) House at Stanford and others who participated in the above-mentioned seminar. It was their interest and probing that forced me to expand the application of these ideas and provided the final push for this book. But equally, special thanks are due to The Canada Council, who have supported me so well as a graduate student at Stanford that my spare time has been free enough for continual research apart from my required studies, including the research for and the writing of this book.

I would like to thank those friends who, in one way or another, were involved in the completion of this book: Keith Gilley, Carolyn Olsen, and Mel Piehl, who read the manuscript and provided me with many valuable suggestions; Richard Schwartz and Pete Winn, who not only read it but deserve credit for continually reminding me to take the most serious project always with a grain of salt; and Alan Miller of the Stanford Humanities Department, who brought his own considerable knowledge of Oriental thought to bear on my uses of Eastern philosophy and religion. Finally, to my wife, Shari, whose enthusiasm for the whole project spurred me to take it up immediately, I add a very special thanks.

B. W.

Stanford, California

1
Chaos or Control

BY ANY OBJECTIVE STANDARDS our freedom is an island battered by a hundred storms. Man is now free to descend into the oceans or to fly to the moon, but such freedoms are granted to a privileged few. We are apparently free to live, but few things in life are free. In a nation that idealizes "life, liberty and the pursuit of happiness," these are guaranteed only for those who conform the major contours of life to standards acceptable to the rest of our culture and society. Those of our youth who do conform must live in a world of contradiction and chance, since liberty is founded upon compulsory military service for a random selection. We live in a century in which legal slavery has been abolished, but full freedom and equal opportunity for Blacks and Browns has not arrived. And, finally, we have reached an environmental crisis so acute that many traditional freedoms—perhaps even our continued existence on this planet—are seriously in doubt. What few islands of freedom and security we now have are threatened by the tides of war, environmental decay, and the increasing controls of government itself.

What we experience, then, is a feeling of being trapped in a world where we ought to be free. But apparently it always has been this way. The struggle for freedom has been a dominant theme, not just for the thirty or forty centuries of recorded history but ever since men came down from the trees. Indeed, a plausible evolutionary theory might be built around the idea that the inner thrust of development is toward increased freedom. But this perspective makes our freedom only more problematic, since we seem to be losing as much or more than we are gaining.

Thinking about this kind of dilemma, if I may introduce a personal note, usually makes me chuckle and sometimes laugh right out loud. I am particularly tickled by philosophical tangles such as whether we are determined or free, and other perennial puzzles such as the origin of evil, the meaning of meaning, or how we can be sure of what we know. Thinking about these leads to circular arguments where the solution somehow contains the problem, and so we can only go round and round.

But most such problems are philosophical versions of what Ronald Laing has called "knots"—a word that he has developed mainly in terms of psychological and social relationships.[1] Philosophical knots are generated when we argue from bad assumptions, a practice to which the majority of Western thinkers have been addicted—though quite unconsciously.

One of the bad habits to which we are all addicted is reading our own philosophical confusions or personal problems into the outer world, and therefore blaming It rather than ourselves. In medieval times men blamed their own sins on the evil influence of the Devil and attributed to the Grace of the Divine Ruler their own best impulses. In our own times, as Julian Huxley has suggested, God is "beginning to resemble not a ruler, but the last fading smile of a cosmic Cheshire cat," [2] suggesting that we ought to visualize him as playfully tangling the world like a ball of wool into One Holy Cosmic Knot. Since all the ends are hidden inside, no one knows how to untangle it, and every attempt to sort things out only serves to tighten the knot.

Philosophically speaking, humanity is beginning to look more and more like Captain Ahab, tied with his own harpoon ropes to a diving whale. This is particularly true today when there are so many stray knots and ropes lying around from former days. Every attempt to clarify things—from Plato on down—seems only to guarantee more of a knot for those who follow. Moreover, the acceleration of knowledge in our own time has only allowed us to get ourselves, and therefore our world, knotted faster and faster.

Any serious consideration of the problem of freedom must begin with the observation that there are at least two sides to the question, and more will emerge as we go on. Despite certain restrictions on our freedom, therefore, the positive advances we have made should be noted. Life expectancy has doubled since the days of Rome, and nearly tripled in the developed countries. Numerous debilitating diseases have all but vanished. Although hurricanes and earthquakes still take their toll of human lives, a number of less dramatic vagaries of weather and environment have been tamed by technology. Aircraft are seldom grounded, and the lights of man pierce the darkest night.

Similarly, in the realm of the mind we seem to be freer than our ancestors. Mentally we have been greatly liberated by increased knowledge of our world, our societal structure, and ourselves. Among educated people many constricting superstitions have slipped away and recur only as a kind of backlash from the demythologization of religion by science. In this century we have perfected radio and radar, telephone and television, electronics and computerization.

These technological marvels have extended the nervous system everywhere, and our minds are linked by satellite to the far side of the world. In our time the human imagination has achieved a freedom no one could have dreamed of even a century ago.

Finally we must note the distinctive contributions to human freedom achieved in America—a nation constructed not simply from many cities in the vulgar geographical sense, but of many cultural "cities"—political, educational, economic, religious, intellectual, and recreational. The term "polypolitan" has been coined for this cultural achievement,[3] a direct outgrowth, it would seem, of the idea of free expression.

But, having noted these expansions of human freedom in the twentieth century, we must make important qualifications. Whatever progress has been made is limited to a small number of people, perhaps a third of humanity at most. Yet even among these advantaged ones, in the most highly developed nation in the world, the question of human freedom is a prime question for our time.

One might start with the educational system, which begins to operate the moment the five-year-old enters kindergarten. For a time—three or four years at best—the joy of childhood learning is visible in the classroom, and then it disappears. Gradually it becomes apparent that creativity must give way to conformity, that independence must submit to discipline.

In high school, classrooms and schedules and homework are structured around administrative convenience rather than an educational environment where spontaneous learning can take place. In the university, the traditional departmental lines and the recognized limits of each discipline follow the specialties of work in the outside world rather than being structured around the questions or the consciousness of the student.

By the time a tiny percentage of students reach graduate school the excitement of learning has been entirely channeled into the intricacies of writing research papers. The vast majority of graduate students know only one floor in the library stacks, one section in the bookstore, one corner of the campus. They are almost totally disengaged from campus life and are, by and large, bored, unhappy, restless, annoyed, disillusioned, or disgusted. Having escaped radicalization as undergraduates, most become too bogged down or mentally tired to give more than lip-service assent to their problems. Those who obtain a Ph.D. can do little else but join the system, doing things as they have always been done: boring their students, teaching traditional ideas, and writing irrelevant and unread books.

The educational system represents in miniature a problem that penetrates every area of life. People are free so long as they can fit the defined patterns of technocratic life. But any attempt to pursue freedom outside these patterns immediately reveals how limited the area within which we are allowed to be "free."

Life is controlled by powers beyond the individual. Highways and suburbs and the human tasks to be done are planned and directed by powerful and influential developers. Work is tailored to the needs of manufacturers, businessmen, or assembly-line production, so that people must be fitted to tasks rather than having tasks fitted to them. Laws are styled for huge industries, for the shipping and distributing of goods, for regulating automobiles. The enforcement of these laws is fast and efficient—as when an automobile is repossessed because of payment default—because of the deadly trinity of Money, Law, and Power. But a case of personal injustice—racial discrimination in an apartment rental, for example—may take months to bring to court. Governments seem designed for those who govern rather than for those governed, placing more emphasis on efficient procedure, information flow, and hierarchical protocol than on promoting human freedom. In every area of life, conformity and apathy are rewarded, while creativity and spontaneity are overlooked or penalized.

The immense control of human beings in modern urban civilization might be acceptable, or at least tolerable, if it produced real peace and freedom. But everywhere there are signs of control leading to excess. Attempts to "control the situation" have, on the one hand, led to the tyranny of worldwide CIA operations and the potential tyranny of the National Computer Credit Center. On the other hand, attempts to control have continually promoted new chaotic situations which in turn call for more control. Keeping the cities peaceful has too often required armed guards and gunfire, and the control of student protesters regularly turns into chaotic, rock-throwing confrontation. Moreover, the ever-increasing welter of laws is gradually turning the regulation of society into cases of hairsplitting interpretation, so that the ordinary citizen is lost amid ill-defined rights and duties.

The same situation is occurring in the field of knowledge itself. A medical doctor, with whom the physical welfare of the population rests, must choose which half dozen medical journals he will read out of the several hundred issued. This inaccessibility of essential knowledge is increased by the generation of unessential knowledge by, for example, Ph.D. students—whose dissertations are supposed to be read by other researchers but are generally not worth the effort. Information overload is so great in most fields that specialists opt for knowing more and more about virtually nothing. This in turn has generated huge communications problems, since every expert is in possession of "knowledge" that no one else cares about.

What is apparent is that the control of life in America is generating some stupendous examples of pure chaos. And, at the other extreme, some aspects of life seem to resist control of any kind. The slums and ghettos persist despite massive efforts by social workers, poverty warriors, educators, and special commissions. Poverty seems impossible to lick, as does the spiral of strikes, riots, urban violence, and plain lawlessness. Urban sprawl continues, along with more and more acres of pavement, dirtier air, polluted water, dying wildlife. Oil spills are continuing, highways are always crowded and dangerous, and population growth is still mushrooming upward.

What is so distressing is that the international scene is little better. Since World War II we have been warned that we must live in one world or none and that ours is civilization on trial. Still unable to unify the divided world, we have discovered America the raped and our plundered planet, and now we know that the year of a silent spring is all too near. We now face the possibility of the last landscape, famine 1975, and ecocatastrophe, thus justifying the summation by Winston Churchill, who once named ours "this terrible twentieth century." [4]

A good deal of time and energy is consumed by Americans worrying about these problems. It is interesting that very often these major concerns are cast into the striking polarities of powerful myths. We are accustomed to thinking of myths in primarily religious terms, whereas they recur and operate throughout the psychic, social, and political lives of everyone, whether religious or not. In the

Western world the central mythology is developed around the idea of powerful contending forces, largely external to man; and the conflict between these forces decides the fate of society and, by implication, of the individual. Because these forces are mysterious and frightening, the myths in which they are embodied are widely shared in the society, and few are brave enough to dispute such fundamental beliefs. Being so commonly held, myths tend to form their own self-validating assumptions, thus coloring even the perception of reality by those who hold them. If our own myths are not very visible, then, it is because we believe in them too well and lack the objectivity of historical distance.

Though few people today believe in the literal existence of heaven and hell as elaborated by Dante or Milton, these "places" have their counterparts in modern technocratic life. The "hell" of contemporary life is its mindless materialism, its absurd arms race, and its runaway technology—all leading to the unimaginable "punishment" of nuclear holocaust or ecocide. The saving vision of "heaven" is built around the American Dream of achieving true peace, happiness, and freedom.

Various versions of the modern hell have been written by the novelists Aldous Huxley (*Brave New World*), George Orwell (*1984*), and Ken Kesey (*One Flew Over the Cuckoo's Nest*); and studiously documented versions have flourished in the last decade—Jacques Ellul's *The Technological Society* and Herbert Marcuse's *One-Dimensional Man*. These have, in most cases, been far more persuasive than the modern utopias, such as those suggested in B. F. Skinner's *Walden Two*, Aldous Huxley's *Island*, or Robert Rimmer's *Proposition 31*. The most recent work is Charles Reich's *The Greening of America* (1970), which owes much of its success to the powerful mythological quality of both its modern "hell" (The Corporate State) and the "heaven" to be achieved: the "greening"—which is to be brought about by a "revolution" of consciousness in the "new generation."

The contemporary version of the American Dream centers on the possibility of becoming free. This is a national "goal" proclaimed in a dozen Presidential messages and implied in every Commission report, and the popular appeal of this goal has recently increased after years of military entanglement around the world. But the goal of freedom in America functions equally at the level of the individual, as do most myths. Freedom is a goal to be achieved privately through both work and leisure, and guaranteed publicly by government, business, and industrial technology.

But here the task of achieving freedom collides with the method, since work is rarely a matter of free choice, and the public acts of government, business, and industry are collectively responsible for the feeling of not being free. At this point the issue of freedom reaches a frustrating peak, since the institutions that are supposed to produce or allow for individual freedom are themselves responsible for its restriction.

This kind of dilemma leads to the desperate attempt on the part of the individual to seize his own freedom. In a capitalistic economy freedom translates as money—particularly under the pressures of inflation, unemployment, war taxation, and increasing "needs" created by advertising. The results are numerous attempts by frustrated individuals to achieve freedom by gaining an economic edge on others through gambling, hot-tip investing, land speculation, horse betting, padded expense accounts, exaggerated tax exemptions, petty larceny at work, and erratic shoplifting.

But in the home or on the campus, where freedom is seen

as freedom of choice and freedom from control, seizing it takes the form of teen-age disobedience, student militancy, radical political action, or outright destruction and violence against "the system." From the standpoint of government these actions are disruptive and chaotic, and the solution for this is more control. The result is a vicious circle in which the application of "law and order" to bring control to the situation merely creates more frustration and a spiral of further rebellion.

At this point it becomes apparent that we are hamstrung by our perception of the problem. The political version of the central Western myth, centering as noted around the idea of powerful contending forces, includes the assumption that every human action is *either* orderly and therefore "controlled" *or* uncontrolled and therefore "chaotic." Included in this myth is the unquestioned belief that chaos can be brought under control by the application of enough power—which means law enforcement and military might.

There are few examples of an alternative political myth, but perhaps the best is found in the Han Dynasty, which took over the government of China in 206 B.C. after a very brief dictatorship under the Ch'in Dynasty. The philosophy of the Ch'in government was derived from the Legalists and was similar to our own myth of law and power. But the rulers of the Han period brought together a host of Confucian and Taoist ideas and forged a political philosophy that has influenced every Chinese Emperor since.

Central to Taoism is the principle that things work best if allowed to work spontaneously (*tzu-jan*). As Lao-tzu put it: "The more taboos and prohibitions there are in the world, the poorer the people will be. . . . The more laws and orders are made prominent, the more thieves and robbers there will be." [5] This means that too many exacting laws only invite lawbreakers, particularly if these laws frustrate spontaneity by attempting to enforce a narrow concept of order.

This Taoist tendency to minimize law, as we understand it, was aided by the Confucian emphasis on rule by *li* (principles) and *te* (virtue). For us "principles" suggests "laws," but *li* means something more akin to flowing pattern or inner harmony, which is the spontaneous way (*tao*) of nature itself. Rule by virtue (*te*) allows the ruler to dispense with power, for "when the ruler himself does what is right, he will have influence over the people without giving commands, and when the ruler himself does not do what is right, all his commands will be of no avail." [6]

This philosophy, forming the core of the political mythology through four centuries of Han rule (206 B.C.–A.D. 220), provides a revealing contrast to our own notions of law and power. What it shows is that our notion of "law" is highly conceptual and is based on the notion of rational "order"—which may be quite different from the more subtle principles (*li*) of nature itself. Furthermore, it recognizes that a conceptual notion of law *creates* the lawbreaker. And finally, it shows that establishing "control" over things by rules and regulations always follows upon a preconception that what now exists is "out of control," along with some notion of "the way things ought to be."

Most people are convinced that "disorder" is a state of affairs in the external world, whereas it is, in fact, a conceptual state of mind. Failing to grasp this, lawmakers generate their own problems by insisting that the world conform to their *idea* of order. The very act of making a law ensures that what was first only a conceptual crime quickly becomes a real one. "I am convinced that what you are doing is wrong, and I will prove it by passing a law against it!"

Once the conceptual nature of law is recognized, it becomes apparent that any state of order is always drawn in contrast to a state of disorder and lawlessness. For if everyone actually obeys a law, its function as a law to which everyone *must* conform becomes meaningless. This would be like a law stating, "Everyone must appear in public with a head." With no lawbreakers, such a law becomes ludicrous. Therefore those who strive for more and more order would find the state of absolute order meaningless. When everyone appears in public with a head it is meaningless to demand it! At this point the only thing left is to declare that certain *ways* of appearing with a head are disreputable, such as having it bare in church, if a woman, or bearded and overgrown in a business office.

This literal dependence of the state of order upon the continuance of disorder is particularly true with regard to Christianity, which depends for its survival upon the existence of pagans. But if the goal to convert all the pagans into Christians were ever reached, the result would be an end to Christianity. Anyone who was then a non-Christian would be like someone without a head—a freak—a situation calling perhaps for pity but hardly for conversion!

Christianity represents the supreme example of man trying to build an All-Good universe by saving everyone from sin, defeating every form of evil, overcoming death, and achieving everlasting life. But underneath this immense missionary effort one can sense the motivation of a profound fear. Ever since Augustine wrote his delightfully revealing *Confessions* ("Give me chastity and continence, [Lord], but not yet!" [7]), theologians have displayed a kind of intellectual jitter, as if a moment's lapse from rigorous, conscious self-control is all it takes to send a man tumbling

into the filthy pits of sin and corruption. This is the idea of
original sin, a large proportion of which boils down to fear
of purely conceptual boogies. For sin is largely a matter of
legalistic definition, good is unintelligible apart from the
contrast of evil, death is the supreme fact that gives signifi-
cance to living, and everlasting life is a monstrous bore with
not much to do and far too much time to do it in. The flaw
in the All-Go(o)d universe is shown by the fact that when
it existed at the beginning, the most dashing figure in Christian mythology, Lucifer, decided to go it alone, thus becoming the universe's first dropout.

Exactly the same pattern is being repeated today all over
America. With continually increasing affluence, opportunity, and material advantage, thousands of today's youth
are coming round to saying: "Oh, to hell with it! This is not
where it's at. I'm going to split for Oregon!" Not everyone
wants the All-Good life, since it soon becomes too much of
a good thing, just crying out for a little disruption, wildness,
pot-smoking, all-night drinking bouts, hell raising, or just
plain screwing about.

Those who feel, therefore, that they are losing their freedom because of too much disorderly behavior in America
will lose it only if they become enslaved to this narrow idea
of freedom. Ideas can be immensely restricting, as when
one gets the mind so locked onto the image of a perfect
dancer that one's feet get tangled together. To guard against
disorder one can identify with the lawmakers or the tough
guys who are against pornography, nude swimming, pot-
smoking, hippies, and communism. But life soon becomes a
frustrating business, since all these undesirable things easily
go underground, popping up later in new places and in new
forms. One is therefore doomed to the endless task of root-

ing out the bad guys, which makes good television fare for *Gunsmoke, Mission Impossible,* or *Mannix,* but is an exceedingly unrewarding way of life.

Those who feel, however, that their freedom is being threatened by too much order and regulation in America can identify with the counter-culture, with its endless train of freak-outs, protest marches, rock festivals, and other provocative activities. This may be a little more fun—if you like rock music and dig standing around in the cold—but once it becomes a deliberate stance taken to be different from, and therefore to provoke, the tough guys and the hard-hats, one has again become the slave to an idea.

The radical and rebellious lawbreaker makes the biggest mistake of all, however, not by deliberately breaking the law but by taking it so seriously that he feels he *must* break it. Thus the militant radical movements, on campus and off, present archetypal examples of people completely enslaved to an idea. The student radicals, of course, usually accuse the college faculty of being so enslaved. They claim moral superiority because they have decided to *act*—and not simply sit and think. But, in fact, their actions are the result of a lock-step enslavement to *thoughts,* to the very humorless ideals of alternate ideologies.

There is an irony here, since those who militantly enslave themselves to thoughts often seem quite unable to think things through for themselves. Many radical and militant groups are thus programmed along courses of action highly inappropriate to the American situation, by ideologies formulated under very different circumstances. It is doubtful if what Galbraith has called The New Industrial State is any longer susceptible to a "class analysis" in the Marxian style. This means that a repeat performance of 1789 or 1917 in America is highly unlikely. It is also doubtful if the successful social and cultural programs Mao Tse-tung has engineered over the past four decades could be made to work elsewhere—most certainly not to solve American problems of racism or poverty.

From quite another point of view, however, any rigorous use of either Marxist or Maoist ideologies is a travesty of what these men taught. The reality described by Karl Marx was one of constant development in which there were no fixed truths, eternal principles or immutable social systems. His was a world-in-process, where every idea or ideology had to be tested in the marketplace of the dialectic—in the continual struggle of opposites and the resolution of contradictions. Mao Tse-tung has himself said that Marxism is not a dogma but a guide to action, and his own method of resolving "contradictions" was formulated as a refutation of all dogmatic positions. To adopt isolated ideas from other ideological systems is to repeat the error of Christian fundamentalists, who quote Scripture to prove very un-Christlike "truths." Mao makes this clear when he contends that "correct" ideas come from "social practice," not from the books of others, including the books of Mao himself.

Perhaps to illustrate the relativity of most of our discriminatory ideas, we should choose an innocent example. In the summer of 1967—the year of the Flower Children—many Western cities were inundated with hippies from across the continent. Several hundred settled in Vancouver, Canada, a city of fresh air and sunshine, close to the mountains and ringed by miles of beaches. In the center of the city a new fountain had recently been opened and one of these children slipped a box of soap into the water.

This scene, most likely repeated elsewhere, was a predictable one, right down to the scowling old ladies with disparaging remarks about irresponsible children and, of course, all the hippies cracking up at the fun. What they were laughing at was the completely predictable horror they had aroused by a relatively harmless act.

Now what exactly was the soap in the fountain—funny or naughty? Depending on your point of view, it was both, but *in itself* it was simply soap-in-a-fountain. "Funny," "naughty," "groovy," "irresponsible"—these were completely subjective evaluations originating in the minds of the onlookers. This is to say that our perception of the world is largely determined by our *conceptual systems,* meaning that our responses are not free but determined by a set of assumptions, expectations, or demands.

In itself—apart from our minds—the world is neither "good" nor "bad." People are neither "sinners" nor "saints," and the world situation is neither "in control" nor "out of control." No one would consider the tight orbit of the moon to be a product of more "control" than the huge orbit of Pluto, nor would anyone regard a violent explosion of a supernova as "chaos." The universe simply *is;* a lot of very different things are always going on, and people are always inventing more interesting things to try.

This means that the world is a free place, but only if we accept it just as it is, just as we accept both the quiet surface of a pond at sunrise and the crashing breakers on the rocks during a storm. Anyone who embarks on a program to smooth out the whole ocean into a pond will find that his universe does not conform to such ambitions, and that the marvelous beauty of the breakers is missed if one attempts such a program.

Those who lament "this terrible twentieth century" are like those who lament the storms, wishing the ocean to be like a pond. But perhaps the constrictions of modern life, the terrors of starvation and warfare, and the crunch of human destruction are part of a larger natural pattern, like the crunch of bigger teeth which every other creature must endure. Modern man believes, of course, that he has risen above life in the state of nature—which Thomas Hobbes described as "nasty, brutish and short"—or that he should have so risen. He therefore tends to regard the possible destruction of humanity by nuclear war or ecocatastrophe as a devastating triumph of "the irrational." But such a lack of perspective betrays nothing so much as being bound to outmoded myths, along with a failure to perceive a larger comprehensive pattern.

Homo sapiens has now been in ascendancy for about 40,000 years, a short time considering that Neanderthal man who preceded him held a similar position for some 250,000 years. Moreover, the age of the saurians came to an end after roughly 70 million years of planetary domination! No doubt some bright Neanderthaloid who saw the end coming thought it was "terrible," and the dinosaurs would have thought the same if dinosaurs could think. It is, then, tiresomely myopic for modern man to judge his own plight as The Supreme Disaster of all time. It would, most certainly, be a strange state of affairs if men failed to resist nuclear destruction, worldwide famine, or ecosystem collapse, but, in the grand perspective, the demise of man cannot be judged as "worse" than that of the Neanderthaloids, saurians, or the recently extinct passenger pigeon.

Similarly, the "tragedy" of our own individual death is no more tragic than the deaths of millions of fish swallowed daily by bigger fish, hundreds of deer brought down by cougars, or squirrels snatched by hawks. Indeed, from another perspective, when a mighty sequoia, or redwood, twenty-five hundred years of age comes finally crashing to the ground, one might easily judge a single human life as insignificant! From a certain limited point of view death is always "tragic"—a child's tears over a dead kitten or a crushed butterfly are proof of that. But from a larger perspective, these things form a larger pattern or flowing design that transcends the values of our little minds.

If life is not accepted on its own terms, it becomes a burden, a terrifying task to be done, an endless program to be enacted, an unreachable goal receding into the future. But life must be accepted, precisely because it cannot be resisted. Like a mighty torrent it sweeps everything with it. But a rushing river is no problem until one tries to dam it up—and damming it only delays the flood. Resisting it by swimming upstream or by clinging to a rock will only exhaust us, but giving in to it and going downstream can be a "trip" like no other.

If man's freedom seems threatened, it is because he is trying to stand on shifting sand or cling to crumbling rocks. With no sure foothold the storms of life seem all the more frightening. So much of human effort—individual and collective—seems like a futile attempt to bring "control" to the full tide of life and nature. And, failing to get control, human beings feel helpless and lost in the midst of flux and uncertainty. But real freedom is freedom *from* all "islands" of permanence, such as the secure ideas of religion, philosophy, or politics. The universe is not constructed on any sure ground, and all the stars are falling through space with no destination in sight and no limits on the flight. To resist this is to be bound by the strongest chains, but to give in is to find the only freedom there is—a freedom that can have no limits.

2

The Ancient Burden

A SINGLE PERSISTENT QUESTION runs through
Western thought almost from its beginnings: "What's it all
about?" This simple way of putting it need not obscure the
fact that most of the serious philosophies since Plato and
most of the worthwhile literature since Homer seek to probe
this question. What is the meaning of life? Individuals
struggle toward the promise of tomorrow. Human activity is
furiously on the move, racing toward some apparently
fulfilling culmination at breakneck speed. Whole civilizations put forth tremendous national effort for the completion of their Five Year Plans, striving to reach the Great
Society or the New Frontier. And beneath it all lurks the
question, "What's it all about?"

Many people harbor a secret suspicion. Failing to find
any satisfying answer to this central query, they suspect that
life may, in fact, have no meaning, and that the almost universal effort of societies to achieve something is a huge mistake. From this point of view life is a Sisyphus story, a theater of the absurd; for if life has *no* meaning—if there is no
"end" in sight—then it truly *is* as Shakespeare wrote, "a tale
told by an idiot, full of sound and fury, signifying nothing."

The problem with such suspicions is that we receive no

confirmation from the rest of society. There seems to be a tacit agreement among most people to repress such doubts, or to utter them merely as rhetorical questions in freshman philosophy classes. Modern society seems much more interested in promoting rather mundane purposes for the individual, most of them through the advertising business. By this logic drinking Budweiser, owning color television, or driving a Mustang brings some kind of ultimate fulfillment. On a broader scale, life is oriented around limited "national goals," such as President Kennedy's 1961 pledge to land men on the moon within a decade.

The more we live according to these short-range goals, however, the more insistent our doubts become. For what exactly do we achieve once we have color television except the same bad programming, much of which looks even worse in color. Once we have landed men on the moon we begin to wonder whether it was worth it. America now claims to have "made history"—a rather abstract achievement considering all the effort and danger involved. Indeed, the more we look at our activities—both individual and collective—which are designed to accomplish something or get us somewhere, the more it seems obvious that what we "get" is largely abstract. Momentary glory, prestige, a boost to the ego, national pride, or international superiority. Do these wisps in the wind satisfy the question, "What's it all about?"

This problem is not particularly limited to modern life; it seems to be one of civilization as a whole. For civilization is preeminently founded upon abstract values. "Civilization" itself refers to "city dwellers" and had its beginnings some ten thousand years ago with the great toolmaking advances of the Neolithic Age, which made settled city life possible. Most of the major techniques of city life—pottery-making, hunting with the bow and arrow, the invention of wheels and weaving and metallurgy, the domestication of livestock, and the cultivation of fruit trees and vegetables and grains —emerged during a relatively brief period of four or five thousand years (approximately 8000 to 4000 B.C.), about the same time as the Neolithic techniques for making tools from polished stone and bone, horn and ivory. But to describe civilization solely in terms of these concrete advances in physical culture is to miss the equally important changes in social and psychic culture that emerged with the urban revolution. Central to these changes was a vast increase in the ability to formulate abstract ideas.

The ability to think abstractly is apparently first connected with what have been called the "irrigation cities" or "hydraulic civilizations"—the first large agricultural settlements of the middle and upper Tigris-Euphrates valley.[8] Forced by gradual increases in population, these settlements embarked on huge irrigation works, which remained as public property and required extensive planning, coordinated effort in construction, and military protection. It is probable that rudimentary governments developed around these projects, that the first organized armies were formed to protect them, and that notions of private and public (or collective) property first appeared in these ancient settlements.

By the time of these projects a number of other advances had occurred, most notably the invention of writing. This was quickly put to use for the keeping of records and the posting of laws. Writing of course requires a well developed power of abstraction, since it represents oral-auditory material visually. But equally abstract was the rendering of the world into the symbolic schemes of mathematics, geometry, and astronomy. Calendars—based at first upon the phases of the moon and later upon the movements of the sun and the stars—were used for determining planting and harvesting times; and early geometry and arithmetic developed around the practical tasks of land-surveying, food measuring and weighing, and monetary exchange.

The simple enumeration of these advances in the first urban settlements can hardly convey their importance for the human enterprise. Not only was the groundwork laid for most of the conceptual schemes that are part of our everyday lives but also vast changes occurred in the mental lives of human beings, without which the abstract, delayed-reward tasks of the modern city would be impossible.

Precivilized man lived a highly emotional life. His daily activities centered on meeting his physical needs, acquiring food, or finding shelter. Closely tied to concrete reality, primitive man learned to rely on his impulses. His life was totally intertwined with the forces of nature, the habits of wild creatures, and the vagaries of climate, so that his actions were largely spontaneous. Since life was lived according to biological needs, man's motivations for any action were internal, just as a cat's search for food and warmth is internally motivated. To be sure, precivilized man developed extensive taboos, mythologies, and traditional rites, but these too were connected with nature—the migrations of animals, the rebirth of plant life in spring, the movements of the heavenly bodies. Consequently, living with these cultural patterns was equally spontaneous and internally motivated, and primitive man simply could not think of any alternative way of acting.

But all of this began to change with civilization, as the whole motivational structure of life was altered. The regulation of public works by government, the coordination of military efforts, the collection of tributes and taxes, the forming and enforcement of laws, the mutual agreements of monetary exchange—all of these more abstract activities altered the psychic organization of man.

On the one hand, impulsive or spontaneous behavior had to be repressed or relegated to a specific part of the day. Sexual behavior, for example, had to be rigidly partitioned from times of work, and the earlier hunting-and-gathering practice of eating all day long had to be curtailed. Men had to learn to pick fruit or gather berries for the group, rather than simply to satisfy their own hunger. All of this required an enormous amount of adaptation, specifically in terms of controlling purely emotional behavior.

On the other hand, the rational side of man began to emerge as the controlling center for behavior. Personal work had to be measured against its "market value." Personal behavior had to conform to collective law. Private needs had to be integrated with the requirements of the whole society. Thus there gradually emerged a new creature: the rational man. And it is here, in the development of the rational side of life over the emotional, that man runs the risk of sacrificing his central freedom by enslaving himself to reason.

The invention of writing was obviously a crucial achievement for civilization, necessary for keeping records, recording monetary transactions, and setting out the laws. But over many centuries the accumulation of chronicles and records created a sense of the past, an idea that time is more than the simple present. Indeed, the most obvious difference between urban cultures and precivilized ones is the sense of temporal extension, direction, and progress found in city life. In the city the pace of life, the continual invention of new techniques—even the regular growth of population and the expansion of public facilities—all combine to produce a feeling that things are "moving ahead," that personal and collective effort has a "purpose" and a "goal."

So integral to everyday life is this goal-oriented behavior that we scarcely know how to avoid it. Thus a child is taught to eat, sleep, and defecate at specific times, to study hard at school, and to strive for the best grades possible. All these living patterns, however, depend upon a particular view of time as linear, uniformly divisible, and definitely headed somewhere. Everything that is done in modern urban life is directed toward the future, toward the achievement of something an hour from now, next week, or next year.

Living according to future goals is part of what we mean by a "rational society," and the word "rational" suggests that any other way would be irrational or chaotic. But the more basic meaning of the word suggests that a rational society is one patterned after certain *ideas* or *concepts*. The style of a future-oriented life is based on a particular concept of time, one that needs to be tested against the real time we experience.

If we ask ourselves the question, "What is time?" we are apt to feel with Augustine that "if no one asks me, I know; if I want to explain it to someone who asks me, I do not know." [9] Augustine himself elaborated a view peculiar to the Hebrews, a view that sees time as an arena where man builds his own salvation or damnation. Despite Augustine's puzzlement over time, his extensive writings, most notably his book *The City of God,* constitute an elaborate philosophy of history in which the meaning of present life is somehow linked to the Last Judgment. It was this view which became the central one for Western civilization after the Reformation and is so widely accepted today that it is hardly questioned by anyone.

Yet what evidence do we have that time ought to be understood *historically,* as a linear movement of uniform hours and days toward some future goal? This view is consistent with our ubiquitous clocks, but these are simply regulatory devices for a civilization committed to this view! Moreover, clocks have virtually no relation, for example, to sunrise or sunset, which may vary two or three hours during the year. Clocks measure every hour and every day as equal despite the fact that time flies or drags according to our state of mind. And while we sleep, time seems to cease completely.

If anything, our clocks and calendars ought to challenge the concept of time as a linear progression into the future. For five o'clock arrives every twelve hours, Saturday arrives every seven days, and June repeats every year. The evidence might suggest equally that time goes round and round.

The idea of time as cyclical is found almost universally among the so-called "traditional" societies, that is, most non-European societies up until their westernization. Indeed, most precivilized societies and those of our primitive contemporaries are so bound to natural cycles that the majority of their rites and myths center on the mysteries of lunar and stellar cycles, the coming of the rainy season, and the rebirth of life in the spring.

Even within Western civilization the cyclical idea of time persisted for centuries. In reading Homer and Vergil we tend to see their epics in terms of a historical background for classical civilization, whereas these works are more accurately seen as encyclopedic poems summing up the whole culture at a specific moment in time. It was Oswald Spengler who pointed out the negation of linear or "periodic" time in Greek art and science, and the limitation of "historical" time in antiquity to the Egyptians and Hebrews.[10]

Augustine's "historical" emphasis was never accepted by the Eastern Church at Byzantium, and it was later largely rejected at Rome. Indeed, during the High Middle Ages, under the influence of the Byzantines and amid the growing mystical tradition, the Roman Church dehistoricized Christianity by turning the Ecclesiastical Year into a mystical scheme in which the entire Christian myth was reenacted each year, emphasizing the "here and now" meaning of the myth.[11] At the popular level this took the form of the Biblical pageants performed in England on Corpus Christi Day during the fourteenth and fifteenth centuries.

When we turn to India we find that the three major religions—Hinduism, Buddhism, and Jainism—are built around the idea of time as circular. Details vary in many ways, particularly between Hinduism and Jainism; and Buddhism has less to say than the others because it sees man's problems as lying in slightly different areas of life. But typical of this Indian emphasis on cyclical time is the elaborate scheme laid out in the *Puranas,* sacred Hindu mythological texts which took shape around 500 B.C.

According to this scheme the whole universe is an emanation of Brahma the Creator, who has his "days" and "nights" like mortal beings. A day or night for Brahma is a *kalpa* and lasts for 4,320,000,000 years; and the universe comes into and goes out of existence as Brahma wakes or sleeps. Each *kalpa* is broken down into great periods (*mahayuga*) of 4,320,000 years, and each great period constitutes a cycle of four *yuga* of epochs.

The first, or *kritayuga,* is a perfect golden age lasting for 1,728,000 years and is followed by the *tretayuga,* a silver age lasting 1,296,000 years. Following these are the *dvaparayuga,* a copper age of 864,000 years, and the *kaliyuga,* an iron age of 432,000 years. As in the four ages of Greek mythology, each epoch is worse than the one before—*kali-yuga* being an age of decay and darkness. But the *kaliyuga* turns back into another *kritayuga* of perfection and delight, beginning another great period. After one thousand of these, Brahma goes to sleep and the whole universe is consumed in the flames of Shiva the Destroyer, thereafter remaining in the utter darkness of nonexistence for another *kalpa* until Brahma wakes again.

Unlike the Christian universe, which has a definite beginning and end, the Hindu universe has no beginning and goes on forever, *kalpa* after *kalpa,* an endless process of Creation and Destruction. This scheme, which still grips the imagination of millions of Indians today, provides a framework for the popular notion of the transmigration of souls. While time goes round and round forever, the soul is carried with it, dying and being reborn hundreds upon hundreds of times. Added to this is a reward and punishment scheme such that misfortune, tragedy, or even one's lowly estate at birth are results of evil actions in former lives. This whole "round of birth and death" is called *samsara,* which means that the world is a transient "flowing" (*sara*) of rebirths that can be escaped only by the realization of *moksha,* or "liberation."

It is immediately obvious to the educated Westerner that this elaborate system is mythological. What is not so apparent is that his own scheme of linear, sequential time moving toward a culmination in the future is likewise mythological. But in essence both the Hindu and the Christian schemes suggest the idea of an "escape" from time—the liberation of Hindu mythology having its counterpart in Christian "salvation" or "atonement."

The educated Westerner, however, is likely to feel that

linear, historical time is *real* time, even if its earlier formulations by the Hebrews and Augustine were mythological. This is because our own myths are also linear and progressive. The myth of linear-progressive time has continued to dominate our thinking, largely because the growth of scientific and technological knowledge has led to an ever-increasing "control" over nature and a tactical advantage over the non-European peoples. Moreover, the two major post-Christian ideologies that developed in the nineteenth century—Marxism and Social Darwinism—were built round this scheme. It seems clear, for example, that the aim of science to attain a closer and closer approximation to Truth, the goal of Marxism to attain the ideal of the Classless Society, and the thrust of Social Darwinism to build a Perfect Society are as mythical as the Christian notion of Perfection through union with God at the end of time.

Calling the prevailing conceptual scheme of Western thought mythical is, of course, likely to arouse the ire of most of the professors in the Faculty of Science. They will grant the mythic qualities of Christianity, Marxism, Social Darwinism—even the American Dream—but mainly because they consider "mythic" to mean "imaginary," "fanciful," or "untrue." They will therefore insist that linear-progressive time is *real,* and its presence in these "myths" quite accidental.

But the use of the word "myth" is intended to convey something quite different. Man lives in a vast universe of mysteries, a cosmos full of forces he feels but cannot comprehend, aware of depths he cannot probe and heights he cannot scale. His mind, even in its moments of genius, continually knocks up against a profound darkness he cannot penetrate. Unable to reach a Final Certainty or a Permanent Truth, he constructs his own. The myths that men accept are grasps at the ungraspable, tales of the untellable, a pattern in words for gulfs that have no name. In the words of Coomaraswamy, "Myth embodies the nearest approach to absolute truth that can be stated in words." [12]

Behind all concepts of time is the mystery of experienced time. Caught in its iron grip, we seem to be carried along, yet we arrive no place but where we are. Out of an unfathomable future, events descend upon us like silt upon a sea bottom, accumulating a richness in the depths of human memory and culture. What we call the past is our own ordering of the silt, or our own rummaging about in the residue we find in our own present lives. Somehow we live *in* the present, yet we find the dual "times" of past and future impinging on our experience. What it means is a mystery beyond explanation, and so we construct a myth. We stretch time out along a line running in both directions to the past and to the future, or we bend it into a huge circle so that it seems to repeat. Out of experience we construct a conceptual order, and we cling to it as to life itself. And in so clinging we sacrifice the only freedom we have—the freedom to live in the timeless now without the constrictions of a past that has gone and a future that has not arrived.

History is filled with the ruins of men who have subjected themselves to conceptual schemes of time. The history of Christianity is the history of men living for a future that never came. On a floating world, in a universe with no firm foundation, Christian believers have confused their own concepts with the Rock of Ages and then clung to them as to rocks in the sea. They have stood upon hilltops scores of times, waiting for a final Doomsday described somewhere in words. Faithful to the end, they have sought to kneel at last at the Throne of God. Less ambitious men have lived lives of "holiness" and "sacrifice" on the premise that the changing things of the temporal world were less important than the Changeless Realm of the Divine. They have scorned the body and reviled the flesh, gone to monasteries and martyrdom—and died for what the future held.

In the same way millions upon millions of Indian believers through the centuries have accepted their lot, convinced they were peasants because of past misdeeds, and hoping for the "escape" of a better life to come. Lost in a maze of endless *kalpas,* an eternal noose of time from which there seems no relief, Hindu peasants have submitted themselves to the *idea* of a future that is uncertain, lacking even the Christian belief that there will be an eventual end to it all.

If this were confined to the past or limited to crumbling religious traditions it might well be no more than a historical curiosity. But the fact is that Western civilization as a whole has incorporated the linear-progressive idea of time. The reigning political ideologies of the Soviet Union and the United States are constructed around improving the future, and both are bolstered by the apolitical ideology of technology itself. Here the hypnotism of "technique" is so powerful that it threatens to move into a "technology of behavior" which B. F. Skinner, the Prince of Behaviorism, himself acknowledges will move us "beyond freedom and dignity." [13] Finally, this linear-progressive idea of history is now so rapidly infecting the developing nations everywhere that it is virtually certain to dominate the whole planet within our century.

Since one or another idea of time will probably be accepted by most people, it could be argued that the linear-progressive system is as good as any. It could be argued, for example, that this time concept is best because it provides "direction" and motivation to human effort. But this is a self-proving argument, since the idea of linear-progressive time derives *from* the increased human effort within urban cultures. This is to say that linear-progressive ideas about time provide motivation for acting as if time is linear-progressive!

Examined carefully, the progressive view of time begins to look rather pointless. Life lived in this scheme is meaningful today only if it will be meaningful tomorrow. But the man who lives for tomorrow finds that tomorrow leads on forever. He ends up living for a life that is always about to arrive but never does. Eventually, surviving for tomorrow's survival begins to seem absurd and so he lives for his children, who in turn carry on the long wait. Each of us then becomes the fulfillment of the lives of ancestors long dead, and each of us will be fulfilled somewhere out there among unborn generations we can never meet!

We all assume that life should have meaning *today*. But when we look at the way society and government function, everything seems geared for tomorrow. The entire structure of most modern governments is aimed at "improving" the present and moving nations "forward" to the improved future. This pattern got its start with the empire-building of the fifteenth and sixteenth centuries; it was given tremendous impetus by the Industrial Revolution of the seventeenth and eighteenth centuries; and Darwin's evolutionary theory in the nineteenth century provided both biological and philosophical justification for consciously directed development and improvement.

During our own century societies everywhere have acquired this pattern of thought, rushing ahead at breakneck speed, struggling to arrive in the twentieth century by industrial development, governmental organization, public education, and technical expertise. But wherever these patterns have taken root, they have brought with them the same problems experienced by their European and American forerunners—and not yet solved.

The ancient burden of civilized man is the burden of the future: the belief that the future cannot be left to itself but must be directed, programmed, and planned. But while each program is enacted, new problems continue to rear up like the heads of some great Hydra.

The public health movement of the last hundred years, for example, was instrumental in providing physically healthy urban environments in the industrial nations. This, along with continuing industrialization in the cities, laid the basis for a mass migration of people from the country to the city—a migration that continues today as the greatest population movement of all time. The result has been a total disruption and restructuring of family patterns, community organization, and moral behavior. This in turn has shaken the psychic organization of urban man to its foundations. A staggering array of mental disturbances and diseases have appeared, so that mental illness is now the number one health problem in urban America. Whatever "progress" has occurred must include the fact that we have replaced smallpox and the bubonic plague with various forms of neurosis, psychosis, and paranoia.

Despite the success of the health movement, certain health problems resist solution and are on the increase. Vast changes in social mobility, coupled with the breakdown of the family and of rigorous moral standards, have led to a sexually "open" society—the result of which is a staggering number of illegitimate births. Moreover, venereal infection is now reaching epidemic proportions in some parts of the United States.

This is not the whole story, however. The growth patterns of cities, particularly the recent shifting of the wealthy to the suburbs and the fragmentation of the inner city by freeways, have helped to produce a kind of "disease" that is neither physical nor mental in the traditional sense. Isolated, poverty-ridden communities not only breed misfits but spread their poison through the rest, infecting the whole community with unemployment, welfare taxation, educational failures, and a seeping sense of defeat.

The growth of the cities has produced more than mere health problems. Crime has changed from the simple "bank bust" to juvenile delinquency, business corruption, corporate fraud, and drug traffic. To this are added new and frightening forms of human behavior such as parental violence, adolescent suicide, and mass executions of innocent strangers.

Advances in medical skill have lengthened life expectancy but have thereby contributed to the population explosion, crowded housing, and the attendant problems of snarled traffic and urban congestion. When increased life expectancy is combined with technological advance, a host of other problems appear: air and water pollution, excessive garbage, and the prospect of natural resource depletion. We are, at the moment, "progressing" rapidly toward complete environmental ugliness and total ecosystem collapse!

None of this even touches the incredible knot of the arms race, with its related problems of nuclear holocaust, nuclear waste disposal, wasteful expense, and the seeming impossibility of peaceful coexistence. The whole thing is a most vicious circle in which every new military installation simply creates more targets for the enemy to "cover." It then becomes necessary not only to protect the cities with missiles but also to protect the missiles with ABMs, develop MIRVs to penetrate the enemy's ABMs, and protect the whole system with electronic monitoring equipment. And still we face the problem of inexperienced nations developing atomic power.

It is difficult to avoid concluding that most of this mess has derived directly from an insane preoccupation with "progress," industrial, technological, and military, and with attempts to ensure that such progress continues. We have not yet begun to think about where this linear-progressive game is going—what we will do when we have a planet with maximum population, maximum industrialization, total urbanization, total military protection . . . and complete resource depletion. Perhaps then we will find some time to start solving problems!

It seems obvious that this hopeless knot derives from living life in the abstract, from living the present as if it were only a prelude to the future. The future in this case has never been allowed to simply arrive, but always has to be forced—as if it inevitably would turn out the wrong way without the help of human engineering.

But surely it is apparent that nature discovered how to manage the future long before human beings started to "make the scene"; and one of the patterns of this management has always been the protection of the future by the prevention of present excesses. And when we come to think about it, protecting the future by protecting the present amounts simply to *protecting the present*. It is this, primarily, that we have forgotten how to do.

The burden of the future is an abstract one, a form of enslavement that derives from ideas and demands about how the future *ought* to be. The only escape from this kind of slavery is a complete release from conceptual time—which means, above all else, a return to experienced time. Once we truly experience time we see that no *concept* of time can capture the incredible heights and depths of the now. The time of experience turns out to be the "only time" there is; everything else is a mental extrapolation.

Like a comet in the blackness of space, the present moment is bright and full. The past streams out behind until it is lost in obscurity. The future—refusing to be created by us —looms out of the darkness ahead, barely illuminated by our brightest lights: a constantly arriving *now*. What we see as "progress" is purely conceptual—a product of our own limited human interests but with no necessity in the world of fact. If there is a reality which we can be certain about, it is the fluid reality of constant change.

It has been said that "there is only one crisis in the world. It is the crisis of transformation." [14] We fear change. Convinced that there must be some Island of Permanence, some rock-hard Foundation on which to stand, we are frantic at the sight of the crumbling monuments of man and the disintegration of our own sacred truths. Yet the crisis of transformation and the fear of change are self-generated: the result of trying to force a future that will not be forced.

It is evident, then, that the "future shock" of which Alvin Toffler has written[15] originates with ourselves, with our own constant resistance to change and our lack of freedom toward what comes. True freedom is release, not from the future itself, but from all *ideas* about that future—ideas that wear down, overshadow, or obliterate the "place" where life is lived: Now. To be free of the future is to be free for now—from which perspective the question, "What's it all about?" either provides its own answer or collapses as a meaningless question. For the fact that there is never an "end" to it all is precisely what makes *this moment* complete in itself.

3
The Inner Prison

ONE OF THE UNIVERSAL PATTERNS found among living things is the playing of games. For the majority of us the most familiar example is a litter of kittens, which spend most of their time either nursing or inventing games. A kitten's world appears to be populated with nothing but playthings, all of which are itching to be batted about. There are tails to chase, shadows to stalk, other kittens to pounce upon. This kind of play is, of course, an educational process which eventually evolves into very serious business in which mock battles are staged—complete with fierce spitting, flattened ears, extended claws, and a violent lashing of tails.

Some of the more spectacular games in nature are rarely seen except in movies by Walt Disney, who, despite his annoying anthropomorphism, had a way of catching the essence of natural life on film. Game-playing would seem to be built into the fundamental fabric of life, as witnessed by the incredible rituals of songbirds, animals in heat, and the huge tails of peacocks. Indeed, game-playing appears even at the purely biological level, where we find coloration and decoration resembling a kind of costume, a resemblance often emphasized by ritual dancing or strutting.

Human beings have evolved the art of game-playing to a

high degree, complete with definite rules and procedures, ways of winning and ways of losing. A considerable amount of child behavior takes the form of game-playing, like the ritualistic testing of a new teacher. In a world dominated by the competitive games of men, women have evolved the games of coquetry and coyness to a high art, enhancing it with alluring devices such as lipstick, baubles, and perfume. In traditional American society where the Women's Liberation Movement has made few inroads female clothing tends toward the colorful costume, the garb of one ready to play at any time. Within the same tradition, as A. H. Chapman has shown,[16] intersexual behavior takes the form of games, ruses, ploys, maneuvers, and stratagems.

But game-playing is more than simply leisure sport for sexual flirtation. As Eric Berne's "transactional analysis" has made clear, games penetrate to the highest levels of social interchange.[17] Even the most serious aspects of civilized life —business transactions, for example, or peace negotiations —have a ritual pattern and a protocol to which all parties must submit.

Fascinating as this game-playing may be, it is often a frustrating business. Trigant Burrow, one of the most astute but unread psychological theorists of our century, once noted the way in which gamelike opposition has infected all interaction until the "play" element disappears, producing an "authoritarian give-and-take that now characterizes man's interrelational level of behavior . . . , a dichotomous attitude of servile dependence upon other people on the one hand, and of vindictive repudiation of them on the other."[18] More recently the British psychotherapist Ronald Laing has revived this idea, showing how human relationships break down into the violent splits of "us" and "them," thus turning human interaction into a confrontation of "props, masks, roles, lies, defenses, anxieties, projections and introjections." [19]

This confrontational quality has its origin in the fabric of urban society, and particularly in behavior patterns connected with specialization. In almost every activity of urban life—the building of roads and bridges and buildings, the making of tools and clothing, the formation and administration of law, the teaching of these skills to others—society divides into "experts" and "laymen," those with information and those without it. Human behavior is forced along rigidly defined alternatives in which the typical human interaction is one person teaching, leading, directing, commanding, punishing, "doing" or "out-doing" another.

This situation leads to some particularly complex problems. How is the lowest man in a chain of command on a work crew supposed to function with dignity as the head of a household? In human societies positions change, as they do not among the animals. The chicken lowest in the pecking order is always lowest; it is never allowed to assume a superior position. But human beings have allowed for variation in human interaction by the adoption of "roles," a technique which signals to others the behavior that is appropriate or expected. This adoption of roles is therefore a device that allows for the automatic selection of behavior for each situation, rather than haphazard experimentation. Like most evolutionary adaptations, it is a simplifying device—ensuring that human interaction will follow patterns that are socially approved for given situations.

In precivilized societies this multiplicity of roles was not present. Precivilized man could quite literally be himself most of the time. In modern societies, however, people are forced to "come on" in several different roles for different purposes. People are so dependent upon these roles that they become quite uncomfortable when social cues are missing and they are given no information as to which role they should adopt.

Like any other behavior pattern, roles easily become exaggerated and turn into unnecessary "poses"—as when a person works too hard at "putting up a good front" or "putting on the dog." We feel that such a person is not genuine, that he is wearing a mask. Indeed, following Jung, most psychologists call a role a *persona,* a word for the mask worn by ancient stage actors. The adoption of a *persona* is the wearing of a mask—the mask of persona-lity. Skinner, following this stage metaphor, speaks of a role as a "repertoire of behavior." [20] The appropriateness of the stage metaphor is apparent when we observe any human interaction involving people in official roles, since such interaction often looks like so much acting. An outsider at a business cocktail party is likely to feel that he is in the midst of some strange masked ball.

It is significant that one of the few cures for this exaggerated form of the role is a literal "unmasking." Since roles are closely associated with clothing, its removal often aids the unmasking process. Removing clothing for sexual activity, however, does not necessarily cure an exaggerated role, especially one connected with sexual performance (i.e., the aggressive he-man role, or the proper-lady role). This undoubtedly relates to the widespread use of the nude marathon in many forms of group therapy. Group nudity involves total unmasking without the "protection" of stereotyped sexual roles. As Alexander Lowen puts it: "Nakedness is the great leveler of social distinctions. . . . Nudity strips the individual of his ego pretensions and, sometimes, of his ego defenses." [21]

The adoption of roles by human beings is more than an

amusing accident. Its importance for us can hardly be exaggerated, since most of our civilized social relationships would be quite impossible without roles. The fact, however, that roles are almost exclusively found among civilized peoples does not mean that they are an aberration or a makeshift pattern of behavior. As Julian Huxley has noted, tradition is "a second method of heredity based on the transmission of experience" [22]; and Esther and William Menaker have driven the same point into the psychological realm: "Psychic life is a continuation, in non-genetic terms, of the evolutionary processes of the universe." [23]

Man's culture has become the vehicle of evolution because it provides continuity of information within the species, in the same way that genes provide biological continuity. For culture is more than simply *physical* artifacts like axes, pots, or boomerangs. Culture includes the *social* relationships embodied in families, brotherhoods, churches, governments, and armies, along with the *psychological* patterns recorded in myth and ritual, art forms, music, songs, and the symbolic structures of language and mathematics.

We have seen how the societal changes connected with labor, law, and government required the development of abstract thought. The suppression of impulsive behavior and the rational direction of life according to the larger societal needs laid the foundation for the abstract idea of a progressive civilization. The very act of dividing behavior this way—of "reason" controlling "impulse"—is abstract in the sense that one part of behavior is exalted to a primary position.

Abstraction is the practice of isolating parts from wholes, of dividing the whole process of the universe into separate "things" and "events" and "qualities"—a technique made possible by words, which are, in fact, storage labels for "bits" of information. Words are a way of carrying samples of reality about for the purpose of demonstrating it for others without the inconvenience of hauling the whole world on one's back. It is simpler to say "tree" than to have to point one out or hold one up for everyone to see. But the symbol "tree" is abstract in the sense that it turns a precept into a concept and generalizes a great deal about a vast range of green growing things in the forest.

In the same way, it is simpler to call someone a "senator" or a "woodcutter" than to provide a pantomime demonstration of lawmaking or woodcutting. Human communication thus leads us to pigeonholing people according to their roles, an act that turns people into concepts. But equally it turns ourselves into concepts. In simpler terms: running a "rational" society doing rationally "purposeful" work involving the manipulation of conceptual systems is not possible if the societal "units" (i.e., people) are mishmashy eating-sleeping-drinking impulsive organisms. The people themselves must be turned into self-concepts such as "teachers," "administrators," "builders," or "undertakers."

But gradually it becomes apparent that civilized human beings are victims of a huge mutual conspiracy in which everyone is reduced to a role for the sake of convenience. The ramifications of this are not only vast but growing in complexity day by day. After centuries of this reductionism, increased by the refinements of human specialization, human interaction has eroded into a confrontation of objects rather than a partnership of subjects. So ingrained and complex have roles and roles-upon-roles become that we have each become what Robert S. De Ropp calls a "theater of Selves," [24] a whole menagerie of masks so dense that most of us are out of touch with the inner "I" behind the mask.

There are numerous kinds of schizophrenia, but one of

them results from being oversensitive to this multitude of masks, as when a person confuses one or more of them with the real face. Eventually this can lead to a competition between various roles for supremacy, as if each of the masks were trying to be the real face. But schizophrenia is only the exaggerated end of a whole spectrum of role conflicts and confusions that have generated in our time a malaise of misery and doubt. Identity has become, as Ronald Laing puts it, "the current idolatry," [25] since everyone feels compelled to scratch around to find the "real self" underneath all the false faces. Indeed, getting all the masks on straight has become a central concern on the American campus, where it is virtually mandatory for each college student to have at least one "identity crisis" during his freshman year—a "requirement" which is almost deliberately encouraged by graduate students in freshman English classes that teach writers such as Melville, Dostoevsky, Joyce, Eliot, Camus, Ginsberg, Beckett, and Burroughs.

When life is channeled exclusively into roles, human beings are "reified"—turned into mere "things" that can be neatly labeled, filed, and stored, like names in a telephone book or a credit bureau. This process is obvious during the first few minutes of acquaintance between strangers. Leading questions are fielded that are aimed at rounding out or squaring up the stranger into a tidy concept with a name, occupation, and political leanings. There is, of course, a defense against this "thingification" and it is called the "cult of individuality": the attempt to "show off" oneself as unique, different, and *worth* remembering as more than a mere "thing." What this involves is the adoption of still another *persona,* but one specifically calculated to create a desired impression. The popular name for this *persona* is "the ego," a false self that is functionally useless except for parading before the world.

The irony of the whole "ego thing" is that it is even more abstract than the *persona* that it is meant to enhance. Rather than building itself on culturally valuable roles, the ego is built upon assumed or imaginary ones. As such it is more abstract than most vocational roles, being constructed out of *concepts* of what one is rather than simply *what one is*. This false self becomes a habit that is pumped and padded at every opportunity, becoming not only one's visible identity for other people but often the primary feeling we have of self-identity. Moreover, as a *concept* of the self the false ego is particularly vulnerable to the laws and contradictions of conceptual logic. B. F. Skinner, for example, applying positivistic logic to the idea we have of ourselves, denies the existence of what he calls the "autonomous man" —by which he means roughly what we mean by "the ego." [26]

There is, of course, a profound difference between *being* human and knowing it—between simply behaving in a human way and forming a concept that we are so behaving. Animals, young children, and precivilized men obviously have consciousness, but they are not self-conscious. This is one of the delightful things about children: their innocent behavior, unspoiled by the hang-up of having to manipulate or control themselves for the "right" impression on others. But civilized, adult human beings have developed self-consciousness—a reflective feedback system that allows us to contemplate consciousness, to know that we know and understand that we understand. This ability to observe our own behavior and conceptualize about it also allows us to manipulate it. Thus we can set up a self-made ego designed to send predetermined signals to others. At this point, however, the whole feedback mechanism of self-consciousness leads into the worst of knots, particularly the bind of clinging to an ego that is only a concept. The result is the so-called "ego trip," which is rarely designed to enhance the person as a whole organism, but rather is directed toward the boosting of that self which is "all in the head."

The beauty of most things in nature is that they do not get hung up on one thing. The endless movement and transformation of the universe never falters. Generations of stars condense and burn, swell and explode, in the dazzling display of a bursting supernova. Continents drift and crumble, mountains rise and fall. As Heraclitus put it, all is change, and only change itself is changeless. In the familiar world of our own experience, daisies and dolphins, butterflies, giraffes, and pumpkins, "do their thing" with gusto, blooming forth on the cosmic stage for a mere instant, then quietly wither away.

This withering is of course the sacrifice that gives their followers room to live—the death that allows for the resurrection of new life in the young. Deer and antelope die, grass grows over their bones, and the grass is taken up again by animals or broken down into loam for trees. This cannibalistic system which has been dubbed "nature red in tooth and claw" is really a most sophisticated system of co-operation, a kind of natural communism or socialism. Like wings and radar, it was invented first by nature.

Like everything else, as Alan Watts has noted,[27] man is not a "thing" but an "event," a man-shaped pattern of energy flowing in one end and out the other. The energy enters in the form of heat and light, water and salt, fruit and cereal, and beef and beer. Most of the energy keeps the pattern going, resulting in all the activities of human culture. The rest is pushed or squirted out the other end in the form of semen, gas, babies, and excrement. This means that man is part of one great stream of energy that "does" him, along with a lot of other things. It assumes myriads of forms: it "stars" and "planets" and "moons," it "animals" and "trees" and "peoples."

A man is therefore not a "thing" to be considered or understood apart from his surroundings, like a bean in a rattle. The shape of his body, or the structure of his eyes and ears and brain, makes no sense apart from the universe in which he lives and moves. A man is, in fact, the universe being a man—looking out at Itself through a pair of eyes and finding out how It all looks.

This means (and here I am using the language of anthropomorphic myth) that man is something the whole cosmos has quite unintentionally been getting ready to do—with fits and starts and blind allies—for a long time, all through those myriads of ages when nature was experimenting with fins and wings and legs, backbones and thumbs and brains. In this sense, You are a Big Act performed by the Universe-at-Large. But most men do not see It this way, since they are victims of the notion that they are each a separate package of skin and bones having no real connections with nature.

Man is part of the rushing torrent, which means not so much that he is floating in a river as that he is part of the water. Survival does not mean reaching shore, but getting "with it"—learning to float with the current. The science of ecology is what this is all about: learning to flow with all the other energy patterns in the river in a great dance of cooperation. But since we *think* of ourselves differently—as isolated egos—we fight the current, compete with all the waves, and turn the natural flow into a "struggle for survival." In short, ecology becomes ego-logy.

Egology is based on the illusion that each of us is alone, cut off from the whole universe—a terrifying game that naturally leads to uncertainty, fear, alienation, and, in the extreme, psychosis, insanity or suicide. But the separate ego is, after all, purely a concept—an *idea* of the self that has been abstracted from the whole organism/environment field. It is a game-rule, useful only in a society addicted to competitive games, but not to be taken seriously. When it *is* taken seriously it gives rise to conceptual uncertainties and fears, like the chronic habit of worrying about what *might* happen or *could* happen. "What if I don't win this round?" "What if my luck changes?" This purely conceptual anxiety leads directly into a vicious circle, for the isolated ego can rely on nothing else and so must survive by sheer ego-strength alone. But surviving this way only reinforces the feeling of being isolated, and the conceptual boogies become more and more frightening. There seems to be nothing left to do but to assert the ego with more volume, like lonely people shouting in the dark to keep from being afraid.

A world full of such isolated egos packaged in tender little bodies of skin is a world destined for trouble, full of desperate games designed to enhance the ego and ward off insecurity. For every winner there has to be a loser, and the egos who "fail"—all the way from kindergarten finger-painting class to national elections—are a sorry lot. Having placed ultimate faith and hope in their own ego, they didn't make it! This in turn requires constant efforts at self-deception, clinging to the illusion that we have "won" when in fact we have "lost." The logic used in such face-saving rationalizations is as abstract as the conceptual ego it is designed to protect. The fox that cannot reach the grapes announces that they are probably sour anyway! The boy who fails to land a date with the local belle claims she is probably fickle. Even more devious is the political ego who saves face by shifting the grounds of the conflict—as when the loser of an election claims a "moral" victory because he obtained 50 percent more votes than his opponent predicted.

The man who believes he exists as an ego, totally separate from his environment, is living a kind of fiction. He is enslaved to a narrow idea of the self, and his limited self-concept becomes an inner prison. The more seriously he believes in the supremacy of his ego, the more unreal his actions become.

Lacking the security of a real hookup with nature and society, the fictional ego engages in collecting "securities"— stocks and bonds, insurance policies, university degrees, and money itself. In a society based on the individual ego these abstract symbols attain a weird kind of practical value, since symbols can be exchanged for consumable goods. But we are constantly reminded that our "securities" never work completely. The bottom occasionally falls out of the stock market, doctoral graduates cannot find work, people starve in the midst of affluence, and unlimited money can never really buy the love of another human being.

It is our commitment to man-as-an-ego, and to the abstract securities he requires, that constitutes our worst danger. The mad race for the security of having more money than anyone else ultimately endangers the environment that supports the whole man, since the rush for money means investing in an economy that cuts down trees, tears up mountains, produces endless shiny padded junk, and cannot seem to build a "better" world without testing bombs, spilling oil, and poisoning nature from pole to pole.

The pursuit of more and more money leads, of course, to less and less real wealth. But the false ego fails to see this, becoming instead more and more imprisoned by symbols. Man convinces himself that his real wealth is increasing because he has "controlled" environments of plastic and tin— houses uniform in bad planning and shoddy construction, offices universally sterile and dull to work in, highways so regularly smooth and similarly landscaped that travel means passing time and tourism means exploring cities full of the same hamburger stands, made-in-Japan souvenirs, and traffic jams found at home.

A world full of false egos is, however, not content merely to square up the whole countryside into freeways and parkways. The conceptual ego needs continual abstractions to calculate its "place" in the universe. This leads to mountains of pure nonsense which is announced every night at six thirty—stock averages that tell the "state" of the world, Gross National Products that indicate "progress," Congressional bills and Presidential proposals that prove moral "superiority," body counts that indicate military "power."

It is proof of the unreality of symbolic living that you can get arrested for skinny dipping, that lovemaking is legal only under contract, that an injured person must fill out an application form to enter a hospital, that being allowed to eat in a restaurant requires "proof" of your labor in the form of pretty pieces of metal and paper in your wallet, and that having an education means possessing a "degree" in philosophy or nuclear physics but not being able to cook or garden or sew.

Western civilization, founded on the idea of man as a separate ego, allows people a mere billiard-ball existence, with someone always falling down the tubes. Believing himself to be a separate "thing," man has lost his sense of belonging in the "household" (*ecos*) of the universe, and so has to "go it alone." So totally deluded are we by this purely conceptual notion of ourselves that we have designed a conceptual world in which all our values are symbolic: principles and totals, priorities and results and numbers, clichés and catchwords.

It is interesting that Hindu thinkers have long understood the dead-end quality of the abstract life of the ego. In Vedanta—that great flowering of Hindu philosophy which emerged around the eighth century A.D.—a distinction is drawn between the ego (*jivatma*) and the self (*atman*). The *atman* is the innermost "I" of man. This *atman* includes not only the unconscious regions of the mind and the physical body but also the Absolute (*Brahman*) of the whole universe. The ecological idea that the whole universe is related to each of us and that man is a focusing of energy-in-process is perfectly obvious to the enlightened Hindu, who would express it mythologically by asserting that the self (*atman*) is continuous with the Divine Reality of all things (*Brahman*): *tat tvam asi*—"That art Thou." Beside this, the abstract ego looks paltry indeed!

It is also perfectly obvious to the enlightened Hindu that civilized men tend to see the world from the viewpoint of the *jivatma,* the isolated little ego that is an abstraction from the whole. From this point of view, the daily tasks of economics and politics and the careful attention to household and religious ritual are matters of utmost importance and reality. But the enlightened Hindu recognizes that most of these egoistic concerns are purely conceptual, ritualistic, and symbolic. Far from being *real,* these concerns lead directly to ignorance (*avidya*) of reality.

From the enlightened point of view, then, the world of daily life is *maya,* the most common translation for which is "illusion." The man who sees things in terms of symbolism —seeing his world as "chaotic" and therefore in need of "control," building his life around the abstraction of a future goal, estimating his place in the scheme of things by his stock "holdings" and bank "balance," his "credit" and his "securities"—sees only *measurements* for reality, but not reality itself. Thus the more fundamental meaning for *maya* is suggested by its root, *ma-,* from which are derived not only the word "magic" but also words such as "measure," "meter," "dimension," and "mensuration." The man who is caught in the webs of *maya* is caught in the measuring systems of his society. Symbolism and abstractions hold a hypnotic and magical control over his mind. He is bewitched by and enslaved to ideas and ideologies. He sees the world not as it is, but *in terms of* patterns or grids that are purely conceptual.

The fact is, however, that the *terms* of our conceptual world are the terminals of reality—the edges and extremes—since ideas of "things" depend on edges, outlines, differences, or contrasts. But the *reality* of things is not found in the terminal outlines, any more than the reality of the earth's magnetic field is found in the precise points called the Poles. It is what happens between the Poles—the relationships, connections, interactions, or transactions—that is important. Thus "things" are abstract pieces of a whole process, just as acres are abstract pieces of a landscape. Things are therefore convenient labels for cataloging the world into "bits." But reality itself is not the *maya* of abstract measurement and divided wholes. It is, rather, that Unnameable Something which has no divisions and therefore no edges, ends, or terminals. It is impossible to put this forth on any terms.

For decades students of Indian religion have believed that the utility of Hinduism and Buddhism depended upon belief in the literal truth of its symbols—"having faith" in the reality of the *atman* despite not being able to know it, believing that the world is *maya* (*an* illusion!), or believing in the progress of the individual through aeons of *kalpas* and millions of incarnations. This literalism parallels the naïve belief that "being a Christian" depends on the literal acceptance of the Trinity, the incarnation of the Father in the Son, and the resurrection of the body. It was therefore thought that "liberation" was the result of understanding and believing in these ancient myths.

But Hindu enlightenment (*moksha*) or Buddhist liberation (*nirvana*) comes not when these ideas have been accepted but when they have been discarded—when one recognizes the conceptual trap of *maya*. Once one transcends the ignorance of seeing the world in terms of preconceived patterns, one arrives at a state described as *nirvikalpa* (without conception) or *nirvisanka* (beyond all distinctions). Liberation from the inner prison occurs—*not* by throwing away all earthly things, *not* by fleeing to a monastic cave or castle, *not* by transcending this world (whatever that might mean)—but by avoiding the bondage of having to see the world one way, by escaping the necessity of holding beliefs or living according to an ideology. Being thus disentangled from concepts includes being disentangled from any self-concept, which means that one can live and flow with the whole of reality in ecological harmony—letting the world come as it will rather than forcing it to come as *we* will.

It is not necessary, then, to adopt the disciplines of Indian worship or the arduous practice of *yoga* to achieve liberation any more than it is necessary to adopt Christian metaphysics, Hegelian dialectics, or Mao Tse-tung's theory of contradictions. These may provide stepping-stones for some people, though they may also merely replace one philosophic knot with another. Above all, they do not guarantee liberation. The point is that "liberation" is itself a concept, and anyone who advocates a particular practice for achieving freedom is, in fact, enslaved to an enterprise and a conceptual goal. Moreover, the logic of following a practice assumes that the follower is a separate entity: an ego seeking something—an assumption that sabotages the whole program.

It is for these reasons that the highest Zen masters of Japan have a captivating gleam in their eyes, which positively sparkle when a student asks questions such as, "How can I achieve *satori* (enlightenment)?" There is no way to *achieve satori,* and so the Master will say something like, "Three pounds of flax!" or "Here is a tall bamboo; there is a short one!" [28] Until the student gives up all his ideas of freedom and all his notions of how to get it—even the goal of freedom itself—he is not free enough to see the *reality* right before his eyes—indeed, the same reality that is right behind his eyes: the One Undivided Whole from which he cannot be a-part. In seeing THIS, a freedom that cannot be said will be realized.

4

The Outer Quest

THE ENSLAVEMENT of almost all human endeavors to a few untested assumptions has hardly been realized. This is particularly true of the idea that each of us is a separate entity made up of an ego packaged in a body. Anthropologists and ecologists, for example, typically describe civilization as a turning point when men ceased being controlled by their environment and learned instead to control it. As an insight into the nature of precivilized man, however, this is sheer nonsense, since the ideas of "controlling" or "being controlled" depend on the psychological feeling of being separate from the universe. Precivilized man lacked this feeling almost completely. Moreover, as an insight into civilized man this description is highly dubious, since the assumed separation is largely an illusion. If ecology has taught us anything, it is that every effort at "controlling" nature has uncontrollable repercussions.

Since our views of wild animals are, like our ideas about primitive man, contaminated by "civilized" assumptions, we tend to regard the nervous twitching of a fish in shallow water or a squirrel on the grass as symptoms of fear. We believe these creatures live in constant dread of being gobbled up—a belief that makes us horrified at the thought of

giving up "control" over our surroundings. This kind of ex-
pectant dread derives from the delusion that we are separate
from our surroundings, or trapped *in* them, and therefore
impotent and vulnerable. It is this idea of vulnerability
which we fear. But fish or squirrels do not "think about"
their world in terms of what *might* happen and are therefore
not paralyzed by possibilities—or worse, frightened by fear
itself.

Wild creatures act according to instinct. Their continual
watchfulness is not consciously directed but managed by the
unconscious—in much the same way that we manage the
beating of our hearts or the digesting of food. Our misinter-
pretation of animal behavior results from "reading in" our
own conscious kind of attention where there is none and, at
the same time, failing to see how fully aware wild creatures
are at a sensory level that we have all but suppressed in ourselves.

Since most of our precepts are filtered through consciousness according to our rational "goals" and "purposes"—
especially the goal of "controlling" our environment—the
idea of living "at the mercy of nature" terrifies us. Aware of
how big it is and of how small we are, we fail to see that this
is a conceptual illusion deriving from an imaginary separation of "us" from "it."

This illusion, along with our strong mistrust of instinctive
behavior, derives from an excessive reliance on reason, and
especially on the purely conceptual notion of the self as a
rational ego. The most dangerous thing for reason is the "irrational" power of bodily desire and violent emotion. Thus,
throughout most of Western history and perhaps most notably in medieval Christianity, excessive trust in the conscious
intellect has gone hand in hand with a denigration of anything physical, sensory, instinctual, or "unconscious."

The philosophy of Descartes (1596-1650), founded on the equation "I think, therefore I am," laid the groundwork for a psychology based almost entirely on consciousness. Despite the subsequent emphasis on dreams, hallucinations, and the paranormal in the late eighteenth-century Romantic movement throughout most of Europe, the psychology of consciousness continued to dominate. When Freud finally uncovered the tremendous power of the unconscious, the fear and neglect of it over so many centuries came to be focused in his model of the human psyche. The "ego" became the vulnerable pressure point, driven by irrational passions and impulses called the "id." Widespread popularization of Freudian psychology has prolonged this bias, as Victor White has noted: "We have come to think of the unconscious as nothing but an alleged refuse-bin of the mind, a receptacle into which all noxious material is hastily repressed, and on which decent people keep the lid firmly shut." [29]

Like most dualistic theories, the split between reason and instinct or between the conscious and the unconscious suffered from exaggeration. Since personal identity was mainly linked to reason and consciousness, instinct and the unconscious was also limited—mainly to the bold and simplistic drives of sexuality. Freud's idea of the unconscious bears unmistakable signs of nineteenth-century rationality and prudery—a combination that reveals itself throughout nineteenth-century culture in the form of exaggerated repression and its usual result: sexual suggestiveness in virtually every aspect of the culture, leading to a kind of "sex on the brain."

Any careful look at primitive human behavior or the characteristic habits of animals quickly reveals that sexual instincts are a miniscule part of wide-ranging instinctual patterns, including, for example, the protection of feeding territory, the changing colors of some species to blend with natural surroundings, the homing instinct of birds and fish, and deeply ingrained behavior that controls the size of the population.

The more we contemplate the mystery of man, the more apparent it becomes that the conscious ego is far too limited to provide a center for the human self. Such a narrow identification is possible only for someone more interested in tidy concepts than in apprehending reality. For whatever "I" am, it is clear that I can observe the roles and conscious ideas of my psyche in the same way that I can observe my emotions and instincts—or my hands and feet. At the same time, the flow of my dreams and emotions—even my thoughts—is "beyond" or "below" my rational control. Indeed, these seem to arise from inaccessible sources, just as the growth and patterning of my body come from regions my reason cannot comprehend.

At this level there is no way to separate reason from emotion and instinct, or the "mental" from the "physical." Nor in this context is it particularly useful to talk about the unconscious at all, since we are easily led back into a dualism of minds—"conscious" and "unconscious." The fact is that all the functions of the mind, all the functions of the physical organism—indeed, the fundamental genetic patterning of eye color and head shape and the continual regeneration of living cells—are expressions of a "wisdom" far more basic than any merely "rational" knowledge. Moreover, this wisdom is part of a broader spectrum of "wisdom" in the whole of nature which was, after all, intelligent enough to evolve the human organism. The distinction between what is "outside" us and "inside" is our distinction, not nature's. For nature is both inside and outside, and what "I" happen to be doing is precisely what nature itself is doing at a focal point that happens to be conscious of itself.

This way of seeing the world is so strange to us that we forget it was the normal way for precivilized man. In his world everything was invested with magic, with mysterious power, with *mana*. Precivilized man saw nature as alive, sacred, and personal. It was part of himself, and his totems involved elaborate patterns of kinship connecting him with the whole animal and vegetable world. These were not patterns that a primitive tribesman would or could defend intellectually; they were patterns of feeling for which the anthropologist Levy-Bruhl once coined the phrase "mystical participation." Totally enmeshed with his surroundings— with the rising sun and seasonal cycles, the migratory habits of animals and fish, the growth patterns of fruits and grains —precivilized man felt the daily pressure of the mysterious powers of nature, powers that we can only describe as sacred and magical. Totally united to his world, primitive man felt no need to "return" to the matrix of his being.

But with the coming of urban civilization and culture a vast schism occurred in the human psyche that led to the alienation of the conscious ego from the body and from nature. The whole social structure of vocational role-playing, coupled with the external ordering of people by rational law and judicial authority, eventually produced a lonely, isolated, frightened urban creature—full of alien impulses for which he could be punished, subject to dreams and feelings he could not comprehend, isolated from a natural world in which he could no longer survive.

What gradually emerged was an insecurity such as no precivilized man could ever experience—the insecurity of the rational intellect in an "irrational" world, of a conscious being surrounded by a vast unconsciousness, of a living creature in a dead universe. Failing to realize that "rational" and "irrational," "conscious" and "unconscious," "living" and "dead," are concepts imposed rather than direct experiences, urban man plummeted into an alienation derived from his own conscious ego. Thenceforward all his conscious effort became directed by the quest for security and certainty. The world he experienced—the world of process and relativity—was a world to be *endured* while he cast his mind to the distant realm of the Permanent and the Absolute.

It is therefore no accident that both speculative philosophy and the major world religions came to fruition in areas of urban settlement. Moreover, the fact that these religions emerged globally during and immediately following the so-called "axial period" in the sixth century B.C.[30] suggests that civilized men everywhere experienced the same insecurity and alienation. This is further apparent when we examine the fundamental assumptions of many world religions. Despite vast differences between Hinduism and Buddhism on the one hand, and Judaism, Christianity, and Islam on the other, the central dilemma of their early mythologies is man himself—conscious, rational, egoistic man.

In Hebrew mythology the "sin" of humanity is Adam's selfish grasping for knowledge, a sin that is only finally canceled by the self-emptying (*kenosis*) of the Messiah. In Buddhism, the first two Noble Truths, allegedly uttered by Gautama at Benares after his awakening (*bodhi*), are that life as we normally live it is suffering (*dukkha*) and that this suffering is caused by the grasping and clinging (*trishna*) of the rational ego. It is knowledge, then, the rational dependence on *concepts*—and especially the limited concept of the self-as-ego—which constitutes the central dilemma of these religions. This is to say that these religions result from, and run counter to, the conscious, rational ego-structures of urban culture.

This is not so obvious in Chinese and Japanese philosophy, perhaps because the intense urbanization of the West never found a parallel in the Orient. But Confucianism, as we have seen, reversed the reliance on rational and legalistic politics, preferring instead a kind of subversive rulership by natural virtue. Taoism carried this reversal even farther in a complete repudiation of power politics, rational action, and conscious control. In the *Tao Te Ching,* the most important document for Taoist thought, we find the following:

> The sage manages affairs without action
> And spreads doctrines without words.
>
> He does not show himself; therefore he is luminous.
> He does not justify himself; therefore he becomes
>   prominent.
> He does not boast of himself; therefore he is given
>   credit.
> He does not brag; therefore he can endure for long.
> It is precisely because he does not compete that
>   the world cannot compete with him.[31]

This is completely consistent with the Taoist distrust of all rational statements about reality.

> The Tao that can be told of is not the eternal Tao;
> The name that can be named is not the eternal name.
>
> Tao is empty (like a bowl).
> It may be used but its capacity is never exhausted.[32]

The point is that the words and cultural grids of civilized man can never capture reality, precisely because it is not a concept but an experience.

Though in principle Christianity has maintained the Absolute God as superior to all thought and formulation— as Paul put it, "the foolishness of God is wiser than men" [33] —in practice, theologians have spent incredible energy on thinking about and precisely formulating this Absolute. Thus the theological God is preeminently "above board," reasonable, purposeful, knowledgeable. If man is made in God's image, this is only partially so, in the sense that man too has reason. It does not work in reverse: God has no analogue to the subliminal qualities of human instinct and emotion, dreams, mysterious desires, or unconscious repressions. He is fully aware, fully conscious, with no Freudian id. To quote Paul again, "the Spirit explores everything, even the depths of God's own nature." [34]

It is difficult to avoid concluding that the Christian God is a projection of man's own "worship" of reason. For this God is the conscious maker of the world—the creator who has a plan and carries it through to completion, who knows his product and loves it as a craftsman loves the fruits of his effort. Moreover, the doctrine that "in the beginning was the Word" could take root only in a rational civilization where things are the result of thoughts, as pots are the result of intentions in the mind of the potter. The philosophical analogue to this emerged in the same axial period in the thought of Plato, who believed not that ideas were pale shadows of things but that things were pale shadows of Ideas. As Alan Watts has noted, "it is hard not to feel that this is the power of thought running away with itself and getting out of hand, and defending itself against the charge of nonsense by asserting that its own reality is primordial, and nature but its clumsy copy." [35]

The trouble with the Absolute projected in the image of man is that the God who results has all the characteristics of the rational ego. Thus he rules the universe in the manner of a kingly tyrant, maintaining authority by unbreakable laws and the exercise of irresistible power—as Jehovah did in the whirlwind with Job. He confronts man as a giant brain who knows everything, who can outguess every paltry move that man makes, and who demands obedience or "be damned"! Throughout the centuries theologians have returned again to the New Testament God of Love, the self-emptying God who died on the cross for mankind; but, because of the coexistence of God in heaven with the Son on earth, the whole incarnation and resurrection has continued to look like a drama under the direction of the Real Boss in the sky. Thus the Lawgiver, Judge, and Ruler image of God has persisted to this day.

The quest of man for Authority and Security, for rock-hard Absolutes and Eternal Permanences, has, however, resulted in a "trade-off" of dubious worth. As Jung put it, "overvalued reason has this in common with political absolutism: under its dominion the individual is pauperized." [36] Living under the security of Divine Order, men have found their justification for the "life of reason" but have still had to live with nature—their own vulnerable bodies and the stubborn sludge of the material universe. The insecurity that derived originally from the schism in the psyche was not healed by the doctrine of Divine Order and Providence; life was not reintegrated. It was, rather, put under the constraints of a new and larger tyranny. For under the implacable Lord of Heaven it was no longer a simple matter of men resisting the lure of nature, the temptations of the flesh, and the constant desire to "goof off." It was now a matter of, "Get with it, Man, or else!"

The tyrant can maintain rule for a long time, of course, if he plays his cards right. Machiavelli's famous book *The Prince* (1528) tells how this is done. It is a manual for tyrants and deals with such kingly problems as "Cruelty and Clemency, and Whether it is Better to be Loved or Feared." *The Prince* was Joseph Stalin's bedside companion, and is still read as a text in practical politics.

In the case of the Tyrant God the way to stay in power was to soften his dictatorship and become a pal to the peasants, while keeping everyone in darkness about the profundity of his "purposes." In this the Lord of Heaven has had much help from theologians of various persuasions: from the You-Too-Can-Be-Saved variety such as Billy Graham, or the Be-Rich-and-Successful-Through-Faith kind such as Norman Vincent Peale, or the He-Loves-You!-Oh!-How-He-Loves-You! kind (who wrote in the nineteenth century most of the sentimental hymns still sung today at camps and revivals), to the intricate intellectual gymnastics of Brunner, Barth, Bultmann, the Niebuhrs, Rahner, and Tillich. So "subtle" and "profound" are these pundits of theology that it is now more daring to challenge Church Dogmatics or Systematic Theology than the Kingdom of Heaven itself! Simple atheism is old hat, but Reason is still supreme: "God dammit, what a brilliant proof this is for the existence of God!"

Simple atheism is old hat because Western civilization has long since ceased to center on the Christian life. Man is no longer a "sinner." He is now a victim of genetic mishap or poor social and economic conditions. The goal of life is no longer the Kingdom of Heaven, but the Good Life. Augustine's philosophy of history building toward the City of God has been replaced by the Classless Society, the American Dream, and the technological construction of the City of Man. No longer do the stars cling to a huge dome in the sky over a world that is the center of the cosmos; the universe has become a vast and trackless void where significant events are of stellar proportions—such as pulsars, quasars, and supernovas—and where the world is a mere spot of drifting dust.

The rise of Science and the Age of Reason have produced the new Absolutes of Principles and Laws, softened only occasionally by a dash of Probability or a hint of Uncertainty. The outer quest of man has become the search for knowledge: the subjection of the world to the rule of reason, the reduction of the universe to a collection of controllable facts. It is difficult to avoid feeling that these new Absolutes are the result of a revolt against the Lord in the Sky —an attempt to remove the last lingering capriciousness of the Absolute Lord by leveling him to the dull uniformity of mathematical equations.

The rise of these secular absolutes and the triumph of reason came about after the Renaissance, beginning with the new humanistic attitudes of the fourteenth and fifteenth centuries. In place of faith in God there emerged a faith in the self-sufficiency of rational man. This began among scholars and artists, poets and noblemen, but by 1517 Martin Luther had nailed his Ninety-five Theses to the church door in Wittenberg, thus asserting the authority of individual reason in religious belief. During the next two decades most of Germany broke with Rome.

Under the rule of Henry VIII (1509-1547), England drifted free, after Henry had wrangled his famous divorce from Catherine out of Rome. By the time of Edward VI (1547-1553), England was so far from Roman authoritarianism that even the Catholic fanaticism and Protestant persecutions of his successor, "Bloody Mary" (Mary I, 1553-1558), could not reverse the swing to Protestantism. Within another century the New World of America was being settled under the firm control of Puritan Protestants.

Running parallel to rational humanism in the sixteenth century was the developing empirical method of science pioneered by Copernicus, Tycho Brahe, Francis Bacon, and Galileo. The rule of reason continued unabated into the seventeenth century. By the time of Newton (1642-1727) the whole cosmos was bending to the powerful equations of science, a trend that has never really faltered in subsequent centuries. At the same time, a new and worldwide transformation in human life was occurring—the Industrial Revolution. Germany and Britain pioneered the Machine Age in the eighteenth century, followed by the United States in the nineteenth century. Everywhere it became apparent that the application of human reason to the problems of life—disease and dirt, food production and the making of clothing, the tasks of labor and transportation—could unlock the door to complete control over the forces of nature.

And thus the quest turned outward, seeking to find security for mankind by creating it, by obliterating the causes of fear and pain. In the course of four short centuries life has been steadily lengthened, backbreaking labor has been given over to assembly lines, terrible diseases have been eliminated. The seas and the continents have been conquered by steam, the air by propellors, and space by rockets. All parts of the planet have been linked together by telegraph and telephone, satellite and television, in a single gigantic taming of nature by the application of human reason to the problems of life.

But, paradoxically, something has gone wrong. Just as men traded off their alienation two millennia ago for the tyrannical rule of the God of Reason, so too has modern man traded off his insecurity for the tyranny of excessive knowledge and oppressive technology.

Perhaps the beginnings of the tyranny of reason came as

early as Calvinism, where the determinism of the doctrine of predestination resulted from believing the world to be completely directed according to immutable laws. The same tendency is apparent in the eighteenth-century doctrine of deism, in which the universe is conceived as a machine constructed by the Great Mechanical God.

Were this but a disease of the mind, which it certainly is, it could be largely ignored along with teacup-reading, astrology, and witchcraft. But under the thundering hooves of industry and technology life itself is threatened because it is slowly but inexorably being pounded into the patterns of the laws of reason. If life will not conform to these "laws," then the task soon becomes that of creating a social order which *will* conform. Thus Karl Marx laid out a pattern for history, a program for achieving a preconceived society that would conform to certain values he deemed reasonable. Marxism seems now to be exhausted, at least if we judge by the departures from it in both the Soviet Union and China; but new and more rigid forms of social engineering are now occurring under the apparently neutral guise of technology itself. But technology is not neutral, since it operates by establishing more and more control over every area of life.

The rule of reason requires that everything and everyone conform to the "laws" of reason. In America these laws are "reasonable" to the extent that they are capitalistic and democratic, though few are willing to admit the incompatibility of a capitalistic economy and a democratic social order. The necessity that the world submit to these "laws" requires the suppression of the irrational, which is projected onto Blacks and Browns, Arabs and Orientals, Communists and Socialists. Within the national borders most of these are tolerated, like some kind of gum in the machinery, because it is egalitarian to do so. But outside, where such odd-looking minorities and inferiors, "kooks" and "slope-heads," "slant-eyes" and "commies," threaten the foundations of a capitalistic civilization founded upon the universal laws of order and reason, they are opposed with guns, tanks, planes, napalm, and whatever firepower it takes.

The completely "rational" civilization is one in which everything and everyone has been reduced to what William James called "irreducible and stubborn facts" and everything is predictable because everything is controlled. Ken Kesey has given us a parable of such a society in his brilliant novel *One Flew Over the Cuckoo's Nest,* where the walls are continually humming with the sound of machinery, and the mindless routine of the Big Nurse relentlessly channels everyone into "acceptable" patterns of behavior. Big Nurse presides over a ward for the insane. She herself functions like a machine with mechanical monotony and plastic precision, always demanding "logical" and "reasonable" behavior. But it is very clear to the reader that the real question to be asked is, "Who is mad and who is sane?" For life under the iron laws of uniformity, predictability, and acceptability is an insane life. Big Nurse's patients are projections of her own mad ego.

It is easy to debunk the myth of the supernatural God, particularly with the aid of historical distance. Moreover, it is now clear that belief in him created more guilt and prejudice than security or freedom. What is almost impossible is debunking our own myths—difficult because a myth that is still central to a culture is believed to be no myth at all, but literal truth. But the foundation stones of rational science, technology, and a technocratic society are myths—untested assumptions taken as fact. This myth is what Theodore Roszak has called the "myth of objective consciousness." [37]

According to the myth of objective consciousness the only valued, valid, and respectable approach to reality is the "objective" approach—the dispassionate, disinterested, uninvolved peephole approach that keeps technique uncontaminated by human feeling. This is possible because "reality" is made up of objective "facts" to be discovered. It is possible because the In-Here is completely separate from the Out-There—indeed, because the In-Here is infinitely superior to the Out-There, which is colossally stupid, sluggish, and disorderly until the human mind has brought "order" to it. Finally, the approach of the objective consciousness is possible because the intellect can *create* order where there is none. If the world Out-There proves to be too stubborn and wiggly, too irrational or capricious, the In-Here is capable of "conquering" it, if not by bulldozers and bombs, most certainly by the technical devices of organization, mechanization, and computerization.

It is our delusion that complete control of the "irrational" —of society, of nature, and of our own bodies—will make us secure and free. Yet when we have totally conquered every disease and learned to transplant all the major human organs, when we have learned to raise babies in tubes with precisely determined hair color and carefully considered talents and tendencies, when we have reduced beauty to "aesthetic principles" and turned over the making of music to computers, when we have our bodies sleeping or awake, happy or blue at will, when we can educate ourselves with diodes on our skulls and manipulate our pleasure centers through a keyboard, when we have finally brought The Enemy under control with the ultimate anti-anti-antimissile with multiple warheads—will we be "secure" and will we be "free"? Will the application of technique "uncontaminated" by human feeling allow for humans who can feel? Will we still be sensitive enough to say, "Here comes the sun"? What, in fact, will we have achieved?

What we have achieved to date is *technocracy*: a society ruled by technique and technology. In place of bondage to religious beliefs we have created enslavement to "things"— to tons of industrial products which we are persuaded it is "reasonable" to possess because "everyone else has them." In place of the tedium of manual labor we have tied ourselves to business and bureaucratic procedures, to the lumbering organizational inefficiency of governments powerless to act until they have "all the facts." Enslaved to data, to mountains of "evidence," to the necessity for keeping track of everything and everyone, modern society has become a prison constructed of red tape, national commission reports, data banks, feasibility studies, Pentagon papers, and contingency plans.

But surely it is clear that this Outer Prison of technocracy is but the mirror image of the Inner Prison of the ego. Conceiving himself as a lonely, vulnerable, insecure, and, above all, separate ego, man is enslaved not only to a purely symbolic world of abstract ideas; he is equally enslaved to the enterprise of building a world that will conform to those abstractions. For what else is the tangled knot of modern technology—with its Manhattanization of the cities and Los Angelesization of the countryside, with its mechanized eco-destruction and computerized warfare—if not the deplorable attempt of the abstract ego to justify itself by carving out a completely abstract civilization? Surrounded by artificial light and artificial sound, plastic flowers and tin art; nourished by nonnutritional food, calorie-free pop, and vitamin pills; occupied with computing budgets and loans, market potentials, and consumer indices; busy with moving mountains of paper from in-baskets to out-baskets and filing triplicate copies of reports that no one reads—modern man has constructed a maze that is a register of his own lost inwardness. Confusing his own inwardness with the abstract mask of his ego, contemporary man finds himself in a House of Mirrors with his own false face leering back in the form of a civilization that is all surface and subterfuge, veneer and facade.

The irony of this bondage is that, like the bondage of religious belief, it is all by consent. In the same way that the peasant allows a tyrant to keep his power, imprisonment by the abstract is granted by the permission of the prisoner. For no matter how grim and overpowering technocracy appears, it is grim only if allowed to be, since the conclusion of its grimness is itself conceptual. Likewise, freedom from technocracy is not freedom if it is conceptual, for a conceptual freedom can be exploited by the technocrat for his own gain. This is the Achilles' Heel of the whole Flower Child attempt at freedom, along with Charles Reich's Consciousness Three. Once freedom is codified and defined in terms of blue jeans, panchos, beards, and loud rock music, the technocrat is once more in business: the blue-jean–pancho–rock-record business.

The same conceptual trap infects the radical and militant "revolutionary" movements in America. The shouted clichés of the student and nonstudent "radicals" who want to create freedom for "the people" by tearing down the Establishment are the shouts of those imprisoned by concepts. For anyone who *cannot conceive* of freedom without seeing The System in ruins has revealed that the freedom he *can* conceive of is, by definition, another conceptual trap. The act of conceiving a "free" society is merely a circuitous way of tying down the universe to a conceptual pattern and thus tying down the mind as well.

It is thus that freedom—the only freedom that is guaranteed—is in Krishnamurti's beautiful phrase, "freedom from the known" [38]: freedom from concepts, ideals, absolutes, philosophies, religious dogmas, and abstract moral principles. Only when the mind has become liberated from all expectations and hopes, all demands and preconceptions of how the world ought to be, is the mind fully open to the way the world *is*. As William James put it, "philosophers have always aimed at cleaning up the litter with which the world apparently is filled," failing to see that "it is a turbid, muddled, gothic sort of affair, without a sweeping outline and with little pictorial clarity." [39]

The world is neither "liberating" nor "imprisoning," any more than it is "in control" or "out of control." The cosmos is under no compulsion to go this way or that, to "progress" or "regress," "advance" or "stand still." These are binds upon the mind which prevent us from confronting *what is there*. And what is there has no "meaning" beyond itself, except to the foolish mind which insists that "Things *have* meaning, or else!" But, in fact, if the world does have meaning, it is true, as Lao-tzu put it, that:

He who knows does not speak.
He who speaks does not know.[40]

Or, as Chuang Tzu said, "If the Way (*tao*) is made clear, it is not the way." [41]

5

The Momentary Darkness

IF THERE IS A QUEST that underlies the efforts of men in all times and places, it is the quest for freedom. In the "ways of liberation" of the East—Hinduism, Buddhism, Taoism, Zen—and the salvation religions of the West—Judaism, Christianity, and Islam—the fundamental concern is an escape from bondage, suffering, and frustration to freedom. The decline of these religions does not mean that men no longer search for freedom; it simply indicates that liberty is sought now in many nonreligious ways. As has been pointed out, the same search motivates the secular concerns of science, technology, and the "progressive" society—not to mention the widespread practice of psychotherapy, which has become an official, accepted, and respectable way of getting rid of one's hang-ups.

All of this would indicate that the search for freedom is rooted in the deepest human needs. It is easy and very popular to debunk both the religious quest for freedom and the modern technical efforts to create it. But what is more important is to grasp how central freedom is to human well-being, so important that man is turning his world upside down to achieve it. The really crucial point is, however, that if the quest for freedom is really enslaving us, what is needed most is a new look at freedom itself. What soon becomes apparent is that the "freedom" we think we want will do us no good, and the freedom that will do us good we already have!

We have said that freedom is a release from the necessity of achieving something in time; it is a release from the inner prison of role and ego; it is liberation from the outer prisons of absolutes, ideologies, and philosophical systems. What is not so apparent, however, is how this freedom is to be realized: what method ought to be followed.

Put this way, however, the problem generates a knot. On the one hand, any method or procedure for the attainment of freedom will be a logical, conceptual, and verbal description of action to be taken. This is the pattern for any procedure, from baking a cake to running for president. But such a procedure implies several things, among them the idea that "freedom" itself is a most desirable goal. This, of course, exalts it to something like an absolute! Any procedure also amounts to another set of principles; indeed, it comes close to being another philosophical system. And finally, any procedure "takes time"—that is, it implies something that is not here now but is out there in the future. If freedom is, then, a release from goals, absolutes, principles, and the necessity of achieving something, how, in fact, are we to achieve freedom itself?

From another point of view, any conceivable procedure for attaining freedom assumes a dichotomy—a separation between the ego and the freedom it is trying to achieve. Following such a procedure will obviously reinforce the assumption that we are, in fact, separate egos. The search for freedom, therefore, simply increases our feeling of not having it, and the stronger such feelings become the more frantic is our search.

Here we have a syndrome that is particularly evident among civilized men, where the preparation for a goal destroys the possibility of ever achieving it. Thus if life is always directed toward the achievement of happiness in the future, it is certain that when the future "arrives" we will be, so to speak, "out of practice" for enjoying it. The only way to guarantee the enjoyment of happiness in the future is to make sure we know how to enjoy it now. It is surely meaningless to sacrifice happiness now while we "work toward" having it tomorrow—foolish because tomorrow itself is uncertain, whereas *now* is the one certainty we have. And having it, there is nothing left for us to achieve.

Here we find our first clue about the "attainment" of freedom. Like the now that can never be reached because "we" are not separate from "it," freedom can never be "found" because it was never "lost." The question is, however: If freedom is already ours, why do we feel enslaved? Why do we feel that we still have to reach it? The answer is that we confuse "freedom" with *freedom;* that is, we confuse the abstract idea of "freedom" with the concrete feeling or experience of *being free.* And, in the course of pursuing the concept, we lose the experience.

It would seem, then, that when we think about freedom we are harboring a concept built up from past experiences. Using our experiences from yesterday, last week, or last year, we derive an idea of "freedom" in contrast to another idea of "enslavement." The two mutually support each other; indeed, we cannot have one without the other any more than we can know what happiness is without experiencing the contrast of sorrow.

In a universe where everything changes, however, it is quite impossible to recapture a past experience of freedom in precisely the same way that it was. A present feeling will be new and different—as it ought to be. It is clear, then, that there is no point in pursuing an idea of freedom dredged up from the past.

As soon as we grasp this, and as soon as we try to conceptualize a present freedom—the freedom we may feel *now*—we discover that it cannot be done. By the time we can conceptualize it, our present freedom has become past. Indeed, we cannot even shout, "Now!" without the word itself applying to an instant that has already slipped away. It is obvious, then, that we cannot have an *idea* or verbal description of present freedom; we can only experience it. We can only *feel* free.

But suppose we do *not* feel free? If we feel enslaved—and if any attempt to overcome enslavement and achieve freedom is contradictory—where is there to turn? But another question needs to be asked: If we do not *feel* free, how do we *know* that we don't feel free? Isn't this feeling of not being free based on a concept of what freedom ought to feel like? And isn't this concept again based on a past that is gone? Moreover, haven't we associated this feeling of "freedom" with other feelings such as "joy" or "happiness," and feelings of "enslavement" with "sorrow" or "unhappiness"?

The usual tendency is for us to feel free when we experience "joy" or "pleasure," and feel enslaved when we are trying to avoid "sorrow" or "unhappiness." But it would seem that the very feeling of enslavement is caused by our resistance—the tension we feel while trying to avoid other feelings. This tension may eventually give way to "success" if, in fact, we recover the feeling of freedom and lose the tension. But suppose we do *not* succeed. Then we suddenly feel doubly enslaved, bound up by the unhappiness that we seek to avoid and captured by the tension of trying to avoid it!

The fact is that we are enslaved by sorrow only if we have a preconception that life can be lived without it. If we are convinced that evil or pain or sorrow is unnecessary, we will most certainly feel oppressed by experiencing them. But where, in fact, did we get the idea that life can be lived without evil, pain, or sorrow?

Immediately we are led back into some of the fundamental assumptions of our whole Western tradition. Central to the Biblical tradition is the notion that evil and pain and sorrow are not part of the divine plan. God made the world and "saw that it was good," after which the divine harmony was disrupted by the sin of man or, in fully developed Christian mythology, the revolt of the angels under Satan. Evil was recognized as part of the visible state of the world, but under the apparent Hebraic compulsion to maintain an ethical monotheism, it was impossible to grant evil any real, permanent, or ultimate status.

The book of Revelation contains a vision of the final conquest of evil by God—a mythic reversal to the All-Go(o)d universe of Creation. What this vision implies is that evil is by no means a "necessary evil"—the result of which was a determined attempt on the part of the church to oppose and obliterate it. Augustine gave official status to this notion of evil by calling it the absence of good—even hinting that it was perhaps best to murder pagans who refused to convert to Christianity, in the name of obliterating evil. When we realize that Augustinian ideas of evil found their way into the theologies of Puritans such as Bunyan and Milton and that they were transported to the American continent by the seventeenth-century Puritans, it is easy to trace the roots of our current notion that we can obliterate evil.

If evil can no longer be eliminated by Divine Judgment, it most certainly can by the application of technical expertise: by aspirin war on headaches; by the use of drugs as pain "killers"; by a social "war on poverty" and an electronic war on the Communists; by a computerized attack on the Mafia, the filing of "data" on undesirable types, and Law and Order in the cities. Eventually, by the sheer application of human force, all that is evil can be destroyed, and a perfect world will remain.

But if we turn to the philosophy of ancient Chinese Taoism, we find a view that instead recognizes evil as part of the total structure of the universe—rather than a satanic mistake. The way (*tao*) of nature operates by the alternation or oscillation of good (*yang*) and evil (*yin*), just as sound is an oscillation of sound and silence. This ancient insight indicates not only that good and evil are joined in a higher harmony but also that we would be unable to recognize good if everything were good. In the same way that light itself cannot be seen without the contrast of darkness, and musical notes are not audible without the intervening silences, good itself is conceptually meaningless without the contrast of evil.

The Taoist ideas of *yang* and *yin* included more than simply good and evil. They stood for all opposites: light and darkness, hot and cold, right and wrong, joy and sorrow, security and fear, up and down, large and small, inside and outside. The central truth of the unity of *yang/yin* in the *tao* suggests that life must include sorrow, insecurity, and fear as surely as it includes joy and confidence. To imagine a life with the negative *yin* completely eliminated is like imagining a universe in which everything is *up*, or everything is *big*, or everything is *wrong*. This is more than a verbal trick; it is a structural impossibility. Indeed, for anything to have structure at all it must include the basic essential of contrast; otherwise it is simply a formless mush.

It should be apparent then that our feelings of freedom associated with joy and security constitute a relative freedom that includes only half of reality. And if only *yang* grants freedom, we are doomed to frustration at least half the time. What is equally apparent, however, is that such an idea of freedom is purely conceptual, since it applies only in the limited realm of abstract ideas. As such, it is "freedom" as conceived by the lonely, isolated, and separate ego.

A purely conceptual freedom is like a purely conceptual meal: it fails to satisfy our hunger. Thus the man who associates freedom with pleasure and bondage with pain is likely to be discontent with his pleasure. He will soon want to have more and more of it, striving either to cancel the pains of the past or build up such a "reserve" of pleasures today that the pains of tomorrow will be endurable. If he is successful for a time, managing to avoid all pains completely, he will discover too late that his excessive pleasures eventually become a frightful bore. Or he will discover that his pleasure easily verges on pain—as happens when the sexual organs are stimulated beyond orgasm. If he persists, the body has a natural cure for this: a decrease in sensitivity —which is nature's protection against "too much of a good thing."

As with all pursuits, the pursuit of pleasure leads directly into the trap of time, the belief that "more" can be had in the future if we can but endure today. But the old platitude that "Tomorrow never comes" is true to the extent that the avoidance of present feelings becomes a habit that obliterates the future. Unable to live now, we are equally unable when tomorrow becomes the now! Moreover, such an approach to life involves substituting abstract values for concrete ones—a paradoxical numbing of our real sensations, coupled with a frantic search for the ultimate mind-blowing experience in the future.

One of the more bizarre forms of religiosity follows this pattern: the deliberate mortification of the senses in an attempt to "break through" to some kind of vision—though "vision" must be understood as an analogy for what is primarily a *mental* experience. Under the strain of this mistreatment of the body it is not surprising that the mind "sees" marvelous things, though the method of attaining such "mystical" visions always casts a doubt on the attainment.

To the extent, however, that mystical insights have something to teach us, their value lies perhaps in their tendency to reveal a world at once whole, ineffable, and timeless. Mystical writings have become virtually incomprehensible for modern scientific man, largely because we have forgotten how to read mythic and symbolic materials. But it seems apparent that the highest mystical insights from every major tradition are conveying precisely that wisdom which comes by a complete "giving in" to awareness in the present moment. For the present moment is whole, simply because there is no way of dividing it. It is ineffable—unspeakable and indescribable—because anything that could be said would be about a "present moment" that had passed. And it is time-less, precisely because the *now* literally contains "no time," being so short that it cannot be "timed," yet so long that it includes "all time."

It was perhaps not recognized by many of the great Christian thinkers that the New Jerusalem of the book of Revelation and the Beatific Vision of the Roman Catholic Church was none other than a vision of the Eternal Now— *this* world, transformed in the moment of direct, unconceptualized awareness. There has always been a tendency for theologians to take the experiences of the mystics and turn them into conceptual schemes. This is nowhere so obvious as in the work of Thomas Aquinas, whose *Summa Theologica* has to rank as one of the supreme intellectual achievements in all of history. Examined carefully, Aquinas' categories for God—his "simplicity," "infinity," "immutability," "eternity," and "unity" [42]—refer to the ineffable now. But his incredible length and verbosity derive from attempting the impossible: turning symbolic terms for the now into logical propositions!

This emphasis on *rational* formulation is exactly what led theology into the torturous problems of conceptual schemes, a trend coupled with a virtual loss of emphasis on sensitivity and awareness. The Kingdom of God, which Jesus said was not only "at hand" but "within," was conceptualized and projected into the distances of time and space as a Kingdom to be reached "beyond" this world at the "end" of time. It was therefore hardly realized that eternal life was to be realized at the *center of time and space*— at the "still point of the turning world," as T. S. Eliot called it—in the timeless now where past and future meet. At this point the Kingdom of God turns out to be, in fact, absolutely *central*.

It is apparent, then, that the pursuit of freedom "in time" leads directly away from it and that awareness of the now is the key which unlocks the doors of heaven and earth. But full awareness means giving in to the present moment even when it seems to contain what we might like to escape. This may seem strange, even ridiculous, to a generation of people nurtured in the rose garden of American affluence, where everything painful is avoided, repressed, or deadened with a pill. If anything comes along that is "not very nice," we tend to desensitize ourselves by boozing it up, smoking dope, turning up the volume, buying something frivolous and expensive, or going for a long drive on the freeway. But the fact is that there is really no way to escape the present anyway. All we can do is substitute the abstract for the real or completely desensitize ourselves until the "nasties" go away.

Giving in to the present also seems strange to a generation raised in a social climate where industry is applauded and hedonism is interpreted as lacking purpose and direction. But giving in to the present need not destroy all sense of direction. Allowing ourselves to experience the nasties does not mean that we should leave our hand in the fire rather than remove it. The fact is that the natural impulses of the body will normally lead to a withdrawal from dangerous pain even before we are conscious of that pain, just as the foot will "hit the brake" before the conscious ego has recognized a dangerous situation. Indeed, survival depends precisely upon this sensitivity to pain and danger. The pain that ought to be avoided is the vicious circle of conceptualization that leads to fearing pain—or worse, fearing the fear of pain until the fear itself becomes painful. But what is crucial is a level of sensitivity to pain such that our instincts are ready to respond when responding is essential.

This may seem obvious to most people, but the histories of torture and punishment suggest otherwise. For it is precisely that conceptual hang-up about pain—the tendency of the intellect to entertain the idea of pain, returning to it again and again like the tongue to a broken tooth—that has led civilized men to an excessive fascination with it. A survey of the history of torture is enough to convince anyone that the morbid exultation of the torturer derives precisely from his own fear of pain, his own frantic escape from it, and his general inability to give in to it himself. Indeed, the extensive descriptions of the Christian hell—descriptions that are more numerous, longer, and more exact in detail than similar descriptions of heaven—are products of exactly this morbid curiosity about feelings that are feared.

The truth that pain can be endured—indeed, must be—is nowhere more apparent than in a mother's experience of childbirth. Scarcely any woman I have met has given the pain of childbirth as either a good reason for not having children or as one of her major fears. It is probable that the pain of childbirth is so intense, so engrossing, so absolutely complete—yet so connected with the very center of life— that it leads to a kind of *ecstasy* of awareness. This is most certainly the logic behind "natural childbirth"; and the universal acclaim of women who have experienced it would indicate how integral pain is to the human experience. In this connection it is worth noting that the training given to women who are preparing for natural childbirth is designed to short-circuit precisely that tension which derives from resistance to pain, the anxiety that develops out of fear of pain, and the vicious circle of fearing fear itself.

The realization that pain and suffering is integral to life is largely obscured in the Christian tradition—largely because of the conviction that evil is not part of the divine plan. Perhaps there is no more revealing example than this of the power of an idea to obscure or supersede reality itself! This realization, however, forms a central doctrine of Buddhism and of most Eastern philosophies, largely because they were willing to see the darker side of dawn as part of the total design.

Amateur scholars of Buddhism have often been misled by their Western preconceptions into identifying *nirvana* with some kind of "goal" at the end of time. This miscon-

ception has been bolstered by taking too seriously the Indian notion of reincarnation, which ought to be understood
as a popular vulgarization of Indian mythology. Such a mis-
conception turns *nirvana* into a state of awareness quite
apart from normal living. Consequently we find earlier
Western writers on the "non-Christian religions" of India—
such as A. C. Bouquet, Herbert Farmer, and Hendrik
Kraemer[43]—referring critically to their "otherworldliness."
This is one of the peculiarities of the Protestant mind which
—having rejected the sweeping cosmic mythology of Ca-
tholicism—zeros in on a social gospel of this-worldly activism as the heart of "true" Christianity. Naturally, Indian
meditation and *yoga* appear to be quite literally "out of this
world."

But the highest truth of Mahayana Buddhism is that *nirvana* is *samsara:* the endless round of life *and* death. This
means that liberation comes ultimately, not apart from life
but in the midst of it, through complete immersion in the
process of pleasure and pain, joy and sorrow, security and
fear. What this implies is that these dualities create suffering
only when we accept one half of them and resist the other
half.

The fact is that to try to obliterate evil, unhappiness,
suffering, and anxiety from life is like trying to create a better painting by eliminating all the shadows and leaving only
highlights—in which case the "best" painting is a white
canvas. Such a procedure is the particular disease of too
much thinking, and particularly the attempt to make the
world conform to thoughts. In this case thoughts get in the
way of awareness and experience, in the same way that
keeping our eyes glued to the map ensures that we miss the
landscape.

Thus we find many secure people who are continually

anxious and successful people who are perpetually frightened. In the midst of all the joys of life—well-fed and well-sheltered, surrounded by stimulating men and women—they are miserable from worrying about what may happen tomorrow or are obsessed with yesterday's failures. Apart from the obvious absurdity of this is the more subtle absurdity of allowing the conceptual and the abstract to poison the concrete. This is not to say that we should never remember the past or anticipate the future. For remembering and anticipating are in themselves *present* experiences—and pleasant to the degree that they enrich the tapestry of living. But they become destructive when their content—*what* is remembered or *what* is anticipated—undermines the quality of what is now.

When the Buddhist says that *nirvana* is *samsara* he is not giving a definition of enlightenment. Rather, he is saying that enlightenment comes by abandoning definitions and giving oneself to experience. For experience is never "of the past" or "of the future," but only "of the present," which can never be defined. Whatever can be defined is fixed and dead, describable only because it is isolated and static enough to "draw a circle around" it (*de-scribere*), whereas the present itself eludes all formulation. Such a present can be grasped only by what the Chinese Taoists call *wu-hsin,* or "no mind," which is not a matter of mental emptiness so much as "having an open mind." The Indian Buddhists describe this state as "without conception" (*nirvikalpa*), since concepts divide reality, whereas direct awareness enlightens us with the vision of a world that is whole.

It hardly needs saying that giving oneself to the now without thought for tomorrow or nostalgia for yesterday is a difficult task for most people. The first step is to see that it is not a "task" in the sense of something to be taken up, but rather a letting go. It requires abandonment, a willingness to forgo a "better" tomorrow in the interest of accepting anything that today may bring—pleasurable or painful, rewarding or frustrating. It is difficult to see how we can avoid this anyway, since any resistance to present experiences only hardens us against giving in to the "better" tomorrow when it comes.

It is the insecurity of this abandonment, of course, which makes us avoid it, even if the avoidance is a self-deception. Indeed, so strong is this feeling of insecurity that it forms a recurrent theme through the mystical traditions, both Eastern and Western. An unknown English mystic in the fourteenth century talked of the "cloud of unknowing," and John of the Cross spoke of the "dark night of the soul." An indefinable, unpredictable "now" presents a frightening unknown, as is suggested by the "divine darkness" of Dionysius the Areopagite, Meister Eckhart's "wilderness of God," and Ruysbroeck's "wayless abyss." In the Mahayana Buddhist tradition, particularly in the work of Nagarjuna (ca. A.D. 200) and the closely associated literature called *Prajna-paramita* ("Wisdom for crossing to the other shore"), the reality of highest religious experience is *sunyata,* or "emptiness," a word suggesting the impossibility of forming any concepts about the final reality of experience.

In the popular mind the "divine darkness" or the "wayless abyss" is likely to suggest some superultimate realm beyond all the galaxies, whereas these terms, in fact, refer to a reality so immediate, so instantaneous, that nothing can be said about it. Hoodwinked by conceptual time and space, we cast our eyes to the far ends of the universe until we give up, confessing that we have *no idea* of what the mystics are talking about. But the point is that *this reality is not an idea at all, but an experience*—and not a future experience but our present experiencing. In this, about which nothing can be said, lies our only freedom.

The suggestion that freedom is already here, now, has an earthiness to it that the hard-boiled Western scholar of ideas is likely to find suspicious. In former times he would have said it was not a "lofty" enough truth; today he is more likely to say it is not "profound"—which means it is not deep (*profundis*) enough—revealing examples of our spatial thinking. But the "profound" truth he wants is probably not forthcoming because of the modern habit of missing the forest because of the trees—that is, getting hung up on bits rather than observing the whole. The modern scholar is so addicted to bits called "facts" that if he is not knee-deep or neck-deep in data, his conclusions are not deep enough.

Thus it has scarcely been realized that Reality is the most obvious thing of all—the world right before our eyes! Failing to *see* this, even while looking at it, we are persuaded that intricate intellectual arguments and vast stores of knowledge are required to attain it. This has been the fault of theology almost from the beginning, and the size of recent tomes in this area indicates that little has been learned over the years.

But if reality and if the freedom it brings are right here, now, before our eyes, then we have before our eyes the "simplest" truth there is—so simple that literally nothing can be done to reach it. What is called for is the renunciation of all theologies, philosophies, creeds, codes, and cults —and a willingness simply to look at IT. And see.

But, alas, this is not "religion," say the religious specialists. Precisely! They sense the obvious: that a truth this simple will put them right out of business. It is therefore in their interest to preserve religious practices that are visible and doctrines that are statable in words. But the religious practices and doctrines they wish to preserve are, as Buckminster Fuller has noted, "secondhand information." [44] They are the conceptual and organizational superstructure erected by the organization men upon the religious experiences of others—that is, the *firsthand* experiences of those who *have* seen IT!

In India, where this commercial and materialistic approach to religion was largely avoided, the truly "religious" man is the Bodhisattva, the enlightened man who has temporarily deferred his *nirvana* and returned to the everyday world. He is thus indistinguishable from anyone else, since he has discovered that Reality is found in the present, here and now. To the Christian, the Bodhisattva presents a "noble" image—a self-sacrificing, Christlike man who has "given up" full enlightenment for himself in order to teach others, a true example of Bonhoeffer's "man for others." But, in fact, the Bodhisattva approach is the only approach to life possible when we recall the Buddhist notion of Ultimate Reality as *sunyata* (emptiness) and the self as *anatman* (not-self). There is nothing to grasp and no one to grasp it, and any attempt to try is based on illusion!

And so it seems that freedom is not something apart from us to be reached—either "out there" someplace or at the end of time. It is, rather, the experience itself of *being free*. But this means more than feeling "free" when we are happy, and "enslaved" when we are in misery; it means letting go of all concepts, including even the ideas of "freedom" and "enslavement." For clinging to an idea of "freedom" and resisting an idea of "enslavement" are precisely what destroys the experience of freedom. Freedom is like love itself: to resist hatred will not produce love, but to cling to love will only strangle the beloved.

When we have let go of all ideas and ideals about the

freedom we want and when we have finally given in to whatever comes—pleasurable or painful—we suddenly discover that peace which passes understanding of which Paul spoke, a total openness to all possibilities and a rejection of none. We discover that energy comes not from exerting effort but from relaxing it. To scramble after pleasure and cringe from pain is to become exhausted soon. Freedom is precisely that willingness to face up to the unknown consequences of every act, knowing full well that were the next moment already illumined for us there would be no point in living it. For all that gives meaning to life as we live it is that momentary darkness which allows us to say of every new now not only that "it is finished" but also that "it has only just begun."

6

The Creating Self

IT IS INTERESTING to speculate on how our world might look to a space traveler from another world. What conclusions about the creatures on Planet Earth could be drawn by an alien taking a walk through a modern city—Los Angeles, Chicago, or New York?

Driving down any freeway or through any suburban development, or walking through any department store is enough to arouse wonder concerning how so many people have tolerated the conditions for so long. In suburban America painted pastel houses are crammed together in a kind of hallucinatory stutter: row upon row of tacky boxes marching over a countryside shorn of trees. At midday most of the suburbs show little sign of life. Only the quiet whirring of aluminum roof vents suggests that humans live here. Out on the freeways there are endless miles of asphalt and concrete, swept by identical bridges, landscaped uniformly with ground cover on smooth hills with perfect slopes at precisely calculated angles. Mile upon mile of oil-stained, tire-blackened concrete passing between slick factories and plazas of steel and fake stone, lighted by neon, their shapes determined by the commercial necessity of displaying "goods," their aesthetic qualities virtually limited to the overpowering effects of sheer mass and height. In the stores are tile floors, illuminated by artificial light and "alive" with music "pumped in"; endless products—hard, polished, shiny—a world of plastic and polyurethane: "resistant," "tough," "durable"; furniture made out of bad wood with an "expensive" glued-on surface; carpets and clothing made from something that imitates something else. The only signs that this *stuff* somehow belongs on a *living* planet are the dead imitations—shelves of artificial roses and daffodils, plastic philodendron and ivy and machine-tooled bamboo. Even the sales clerks, moving among the full shelves amid the mechanical bells of cash registers, look like automated robots, lost and insignificant among the toys and trinkets towering above their heads.

What kind of beings have made this world? The question is terribly real since it is clear that most of it would not have been made by anyone except for money, could not be sold to anyone without some kind of "hard" or "soft" sell, and in any case is not helpful for survival, for happiness—for anything. Materialistic it is, yet it lacks the barest hint that the men who made it have any love, respect, or "feel" for matter itself. If anything, our consumer technology looks like a gigantic attempt to "conquer" matter by turning it into something "im-material"—a kind of pure transcendent glitter. Unable to "get with" real shapes and textures, we have constructed a technical civilization that is all "beautiful lines," "sweeping curves," and "modern design"—a completely abstract world.

If there is a symbol for this, it is the *Playboy* Playmate—an exactly proportioned "bunny" made up of abstractly "perfect" parts such as breasts and buttocks and thighs—the plastic dolly who is not valued as a human being of flesh and blood but for having all her "stuff in the right places."

Her body is a "pose" with absurd props; her biography is a series of pseudo events, clichés, and puns carefully designed to radiate Sybaritic promiscuity. Here is the latest Miss July, photographed in the grass somewhere "in the rugged rockies around denver"—Heather, the "trail-blazing bunny":

> Alone and off the beaten trail, Heather settles down to enjoy the warm day and the soft grass. "I really like to get away and just sit. Not to think about anything in particular, just to relax in the mountain air." This day is pleasant enough [naturally] for her to stretch out for an allover tan before she bikes back [on her off-road minibike] to the boys [who help load and unload her bike, but are mysteriously absent during the photographing] for the ride into town and her evening stint as a Bunny at the Denver Playboy Club.[45]

The world we have constructed with its slick and abstract parodies of materialism is an index of what we are and how we see ourselves. Knowing ourselves only as isolated, lonely, and alienated egos, we have tried to build "meaningful" surroundings, a tangible and unmistakable "record" of our accomplishments and control. But as a record, everything we have *done* is in the past and therefore fails to connect with the living moment. Moreover, the world we have built is made of "matter"—that base, brute, dead, intractable muck out of the ground which we value only when it is "made" into something functional. This view of "matter" is the view of the rational intellect which, having elevated gray matter to the purple, believes that everything intelligent is in the head, and that the rest of nature, including the human body is, in T. S. Eliot's phrase, a wasteland of "stony rubbish." [46] It seems clear that if men had a vestige of wonder about things, a shred of feeling for the awesome creativity of so-called "brute matter," they would never have done with it the things they have.

The modern technological transformation of matter is based on four centuries of exacting science, especially the conceptual devices of reducing natural processes to mechanistic models and mathematical equations. Such practices are based on a view of the world as dead: a sort of coal-mine world that is all shapes, spaces, and masses, with no color, sounds, smells, or tastes, and valuable only for what can be "got out of it."

But the technological revolution was possible only because men had already allowed the natural world to "die" —by handing over all "life" and "spirit" to the Godhead. Had the Western God been *integral* to the world, nature would have retained its life, but, since he was allowed to recede into the distance, he was soon irrelevant and then himself "dead." What he left behind was a dead world, an accidental, blind thunderstorm of rattling atoms, valuable only when molded into something "useful" in the crucible, the forge, or the factory.

The "creation" of the world was therefore handed over from the Godhead to mankind, since the original job was no longer regarded as satisfactory. But this new power was not able to solve the loneliness of man precisely because manipulating and bulldozing the world is based on the assumption that nature is dead—an assumption that only reinforces the loneliness. Thus, for centuries, for ten thousand years, beginning with dams and walls in ancient neolithic cities, teams of lonely, frightened egos have been hauling and hammering, desperately trying to build a civilization that will at last relieve them of their loneliness and turn them free.

What we have now achieved is a knowledge of how

lonely we really are, how hopeless that loneliness is among uncountable hurtling galaxies or, for that matter, under the glaring lights amid the crowds and the noise. We have discovered that the whole vast edifice of mankind comes unglued if the one person we love goes away. If we have managed a cure for this, it is the technical ability to end it all in any one of a dozen bizarre ways—with A-bombs or H-bombs, or by the slow poisoning of ourselves with pesticides, herbicides, and hydrocarbons, or by the insanity of overpopulation and ecocide.

If there is anything to discover that can release us from our loneliness and set us free, it is the fact that we *can* create, we *do* create, we *are* creating the world. It is the discovery that "we" are not a separate little "me" in a package of skin, but that we are an organism/environment whole that stretches from the depths of the unconscious to the heights of the outermost stars. But to say this is not to set forth an idea to be grasped, except perhaps as an aid to an experience we must feel, for unless it is worked into the very fabric of our being, it remains just one more concept among many.

The idea that we are creating the world is virtually impossible for most of us to grasp, largely because we are accustomed to seeing things the other way around. Because of a very crude popularization of evolutionary ideas we have all become accustomed to the notion that the world has created us. Because of the "pressures" of the environment, mammals and prehominids were slowly shaped and molded by nature until, after many millions of years, they turned into men. Like Adam, man was molded out of matter by forces beyond himself. This, which we might call the Clay Figurine theory of evolution, is, like its Biblical counterpart, so much fanciful mythology. The reason it was so

successful in the nineteenth century is that it disturbed none
of the prevailing assumptions of the age of rationalism. The
origin of species and the descent of man could be explained
in terms of linear, mechanical, cause and effect principles—
the accidental prodding of the environment upon the malle-
able stuff of living matter.

This general idea of the relationship of man to his surroundings persists and is daily bolstered by technology.
Thus man is a "product" of his surroundings, a "victim" of
circumstances, pushed around willy-nilly by huge forces
over which he has no control. The universe is, in this view,
"nothing but" a lot of stuff spinning about in space, and
man but an "accidental collocation of atoms"—to use Bertrand Russell's phrase.[47] If man was "made" by this universe, it was either an "accident" or a "mistake," not to be
repeated, which means that all we are left with is, as Dylan
Thomas puts it, to "rage, rage against the dying of the
light." [48]

If ecology has shown us anything, however, it is that
every organism is part of a larger whole called an ecosystem, so that anything the organism does has reverberations
everywhere else. We have come to see that man is a tempo-
rary shape assumed by the flowing energy of nature, like the
shape a river takes in a waterfall—a fairly constant form
with ever-changing content. Man is a living process, a tem-
porary focusing of minerals from the soil and salt from the
sea, water flowing from the mountains and air circulating in
his blood. Together, man-and-his-surroundings forms a
Whole for which we have no name.

From one aspect it is absurd to have to point this out. It
should be obvious that man is connected to his surroundings and that the universe cannot be simply "dead" matter,
since this would mean that "life" is a special form of

"death." Indeed, the idea that the universe is dead and man a frightened spark of intellect roving about on a cold rock flung out from the stars is as absurd as thinking that grapes grow on thistles or that pumpkins spring from stones. A universe that gives rise to intelligence is an intelligent universe, even if that intelligence does not reside in cosmic nerves and brains. To *think* of the energy that has made us as "blind" or "accidental" is to imply that we too are blind, and the thought itself an accident!

An ecological perspective therefore makes it plain that we are not simply an ego in a physical body isolated from nature. Without precise environmental conditions we would die within a few seconds, and without any environmental input we would go berserk in a few hours, since the mind simply cannot feed on its own thoughts any more than the body can survive on its own fat.

But what precisely am I, then? Am "I" some innermost little eeny-weeny somewhere "inside" my body and "behind" my eyes, looking out through them at the world? The fact that "I" seem to adopt a role like a costume and personality like a mask might suggest that "I" am the "eye" behind the eyeholes. At times things seem this way, as when I look at my hands and feet, which look like part of the "outside" world. Indeed, one of the few clues I have that my body is different from other bodies is that I cannot see its head! But if my body is "out there," maybe my mind is out there too. Maybe "I" simply watch the wiggles on my brain from afar as I might look at a movie. Perhaps "I" am not "in" the universe at all, but simply looking at it from the "outside" through an ingenious set of peepholes provided by a body called Barry Wood.

This line of reasoning has some "logic" to it, and probably lies behind claims made by certain psychic persons who believe they can "leave" their bodies and watch "themselves" from afar. But such a claim creates incredible problems. Who is the "I" behind the "eye" that looks through my eyes? In other words, who is inside the head of the little man inside my head? Moreover, the whole argument collapses as nonsense as soon as "I" get hungry or someone kicks "me" in the shins. Immediately it becomes painfully obvious that "I" am very much hooked up with what is "out there." The question is, How much of what is "out there" is hooked up with me?

To put the question this way, however, is to assume a division between "out there" and "in here"—which is the assumption again of objective consciousness. The point is that "I" am so connected to my surroundings that "out there" ceases to be a meaningful category. In terms of perception and cognition, what is generally regarded as "out there" is equally a state of my nervous system "in here," which is to say that there is no "objectivity" but only degrees of "subjectivity." To put this another way, my *total* environment is the universe, and the universe is all "inside": it has no "outside." Everything I can possibly see or know about the universe—including galaxies billions of light-years away that have not yet been discovered—can be seen, known, or discovered only on the *inside* of the universe. But this is only another way of talking about "me," for everything "I" see or know, imagine, "fantasize," or think happens "inside" me. It is simply impossible to conceive of anything "outside" myself, since the very act of conceiving it means it is "inside." Thus it is largely convention that we say the mind happens inside the universe rather than that the universe happens inside the mind.

The usual accusation of this is that it is a form of solipsism or Berkeleyan idealism, implying that we have de-

nied the existence of the world and turned everything into
ideas in the mind. But we have done nothing of the kind; we
have simply noted that it is impossible to consider the observable universe in isolation from the observer—unless it
be by doing away with the observer, which means to cease
all observation!

The tough-minded "empirical" scientist or "practical"
engineer, who likes to think of himself, *objectively,* as quite
capable of "mastering" his world, is likely to balk at this approach to his precious "reality"—which he is convinced can
be sliced, weighed, poured, categorized, and "made" into
whatever he chooses. But, in fact, he is not doing what he
thinks at all, or rather, his doing is *mainly* thinking—that
is, applying his conceptual grids to a reality he believes is
separate from himself. When an engineer has turned raw
iron into steel pots or a natural valley into a terraced
suburb, he has simply altered nature to conform to a conceptual grid, which he identifies with "order," "development," or "productivity." But this new "order" only seems
like "mastery" and only looks like "control" because it con-
forms to his grids and because it seems to have been done to
something "outside" himself. But, in fact, it is not "outside"
him. The natural process he has altered includes and contains him, and the engineering project in the end remakes
the engineer.

We are, then, constructed out of our surroundings—our
highways and buildings and computers—and no less so if
we fail to see them as related to us. Our consciousness is full
of our urban environment; our behavior is elicited by our
timetables and machinery. Failing to grasp this only makes
the effects more insidious, as we become the victims of our
own bad engineering. To this extent the behavioral tech-
nologist is correct, since he sees the integral relationship of

man-and-his-environment; and the technological and ecological mess we have made is proof of our own bad assumptions.

Once we begin to sense these ecological relationships the
way is open for feeling the world in a completely different
manner. It becomes apparent that the greatest *maya* of all is
the division of the world into insides and outsides—a mis-
measurement of reality that may come down, in the last
analysis, to the basic conceptual measuring device: words
themselves. The grammar of most "civilized" people—or at
least those who have infected everyone else with what is
called "civilization"—is Indo-European grammar, which is
made up of subjects (insides) and objects (outsides).
Moreover, the primary part of speech is the noun, a linguistic measurement for an isolated "thing" with definite content and clear edges. When we add to this the complete lack
of any concept for the total inside/outside process, the roots
of *maya* are clear.

When we feel through and beyond the *maya* of our
purely conceptual grids it becomes clear that we are creating the world as surely as it is creating us—that we are, in
fact, as necessary to the universe as the universe is necessary for us. In the same way that *yin* and *yang* are mutually
supportive, "we" and our "surroundings" are as dependent
upon each other as fronts are dependent upon backs—one
cannot remove the "back" without at the same time removing the "front." But the Western mind, schooled as it is in
the conventions of objective consciousness, finds it virtually
impossible to see that this universe is incomprehensible
apart from living beings.

The logic and limitations of these objective assumptions
can be made clear if we consider what happens when we
hear a sound—let us say, for example, the sound of drum-

beats. It is clear that the skin of a drum does not *have* vibrations; nor does a drumstick waved about in the air. If the two are brought together, it is equally clear that the stick will evoke vibrations from the drumskin. Our objective assumptions lead us to think this way—that the stick *causes* the vibrations. But it is equally true to say that the vibrations are the result of what the drumskin *does with* the stick!

Given the vibrations of the drumskin and drumstick, it is clear that there is no *sound* until a hearing organism is brought within earshot—and then the organism and the vibrations together evoke the sound of drumbeats. In other words, the "sound of drumbeats" arises when a conjunction of a drumskin, a drumstick, and a hearing organism occurs.

But now if we ask, "What is necessary for the sound of drumbeats?" the limitations of objectivity become apparent. The typical answer will be, "Drumsticks and a drum." The objective mind not only overlooks the necessity of a hearing organism in the picture but also resists the idea that removing the hearing organism means removing the sound. The argument usually is that drumsticks and a drum will make a "sound"—even if there is no one around to hear it! But it seems obvious that it is the listener himself who is "sounding" the drumbeats, along with the drumsticks and the drum itself.

Once this is grasped it becomes apparent that the stars and galaxies drifting through trackless miles of space for millions of years were locked in an inconceivable darkness until there were eyes to see them. Yet even "space" and "darkness" cannot apply before the "stars" were seen, since space makes no sense without the opposition of solids and darkness depends on the contrast of light. The "darkness" of the universe was therefore a darkness beyond all contrasts—even the contrast of light and darkness—an impenetrable non-darkness beyond all imagining.

Again, there is a temptation to say, "But there was light from the stars—there was simply no one to see it!" But light is not just "there." Whatever IT is that *is* "there" is impossible to know—and "light" is only the way IT looks in our visual system, just as "sound" is the way IT feels in our auditory system. Thus we cannot even say the stars were "out there" vibrating in their non-darkness, for "vibrations" are how IT feels to an organ of touch. Even the idea of "stars" in "space" is problematic since they are visible extremes or terminals of a total stars/space process. Thus none of our *terms* (such as "stars" and "space") mean anything if there is no organism to perceive the *terminals*. This is not to deny that there is anything "out there"; it is rather to say that this "thereness" is impossible to understand apart from the "hereness" of our own looking and hearing and touching.

Once this is seen, a whole new vision of the world opens up—a world created by our own presence in it. It is the eyes of man that evoke the stars, and the blackness between the stars, from that incredible non-darkness; it is the eyes of man that call forth the light of the sun. It is our own looking that is "blueing" the sky and "greening" the trees, our own hearing that is "sounding" the waves and the wind, and our own touch that "softens" the petals, "hardens" the rocks, or "wets" the summer rain. The universe is there like a huge Rorschach blot—a gigantic gestalt that is all "ground" and no "figure"—beyond all categories of light and dark, sound and silence, space and solid, even being and nonbeing. There is literally no way we can "get at" IT, other than to create it our own way in our seeing and hearing and touching. Man himself is, then, the figure that gives meaning to the whole gestalt. A spectacular display of pomp and glitter on the nervous cells of our bodies—the world is brought out of the void within the self of man.

Thus the world is to us what we "put on" IT. A dog is unable to "put on" a third dimension and so is unable to interpret a photograph of itself. The same is true of a pre-literate native who, confronted with a movie, sees only moving shapes on a two-dimensional screen.[49] A man who acquires sight after being blind from birth does not know what to "put on" the world, and so can "see" nothing for a time.

But this does not mean that those who *can* see know what to "put on." For we are all the time straining at the world, like looking into the shadows on the dark side of the road and making guesses as to what IT all means. The history of philosophy and science is not only a record of our guesses but also an index of how "controversial" IT is. Moreover, if we add the history of religion and those more recent arrivals, psychology and psychiatry, we find that our Rorschach-blot world has been the brunt of an extremely funny parade of "put ons": gods and devils, angels and archangels, nymphs and satyrs, fates and furies, limbo and purgatory, destiny, providence, grace, luck, hell, chance, humors and ether and phlogiston, astral auras, ghosts, spirits, gremlins and fairies, ids, superegos, the shadow and the anima, the unconscious—and the ego.

The feeling of being imprisoned is largely a matter of being "put on" by our own conceptual grids, that is, having such devices as the "ego" backfire in our faces. It is perfectly clear that the whole question of freedom as it is usually discussed is debated within the framework of the ego-and-the-world, or the "in here" and the "out there." The result is that the "in here" is either a focal point completely determined by "out there" forces of the environment, as Skinner suggests, or else the "in here" freedom is so tiny as to be negligible, as Reich's analysis of the Corporate State would seem to suggest.[50] The interminable undergraduate discussion of Free Will versus Determinism falls into this pattern, and boils down to something like, "How can poor little me in here be free when I am determined by all the Awful Awfuls out there?"

But this question needs to be replaced by another: "How can such a question even be asked?" And if the Awful Awfuls "out there" are primarily products of the way I see them, it becomes clear that a third question is in order: "How can we be anything but free?"

If, then, the feeling of being enslaved is our own thinking, it is clear that we are free to become enslaved, in the same way that a democracy is free to vote a dictator into government. It is true, of course, that there are many people whose situation in life looks to us like enslavement—disadvantaged children in the urban ghetto, political dissenters who are jailed, the poor in an affluent society. Yet such enslavement depends on the tacit agreement of both the "imprisoned" and the "free" that man is *an ego* and is therefore enslaved by precisely these conditions. To be imprisoned by the ghetto, the political system, economic conditions—even jail itself—is still to be imprisoned by ideas and attitudes. Nowhere is this so clear as in Thoreau's famous essay on "Civil Disobedience," where he describes being jailed for refusing to pay a poll tax:

> As I stood considering the walls of solid stone, two or three feet thick, . . . I could not help being struck with the foolishness of that institution which treated me as if I were mere flesh and blood and bones, to be locked up. . . . I saw that, if there was a wall of

stone between me and my townsmen, there was a
still more difficult one to climb or break through before they could get to be as free as I was.[51]

This is not to imply that imprisonment is an illusion. Jail
is one of those terrible forms of bondage inflicted by men
upon other men. But every form of intended bondage also
imprisons the prisonkeeper, who must forever enslave himself to standing guard. Indeed, this is true of every form
of behavior predicated on man-as-ego: the farther the
supposed "freedom" of the ego to exploit is pushed, the
more bound it becomes. Thus a civilization built on the
premise of the individual ego is a civilization enslaved to
the daily task of maintaining a precarious control. Power
erected on the authority of one group over another is power
enslaved to a constant fear of anarchy. Mastery over nature
aimed at a constantly expanding arena of control is mastery
enslaved to the endless task of cleaning out its own stables.
And meanwhile, the slave, the underdog, the prisoner, still
retains the choice of rage or acceptance—the power of winning by not resisting. Therein lies his own surpassing freedom.

Thus the question of freedom comes at last to the question of what we will do with our surroundings, no matter
what those surroundings may be. And what we do with
them, no matter whether we do it with wisdom or with
foolishness, is still what *we* do with them—or rather, what
we do with ourselves. For the world is our body, a part of
our-selves we cannot do without. It is our context, so completely so that it is meaningless to imagine ourselves without
that context. But it is equally meaningless to imagine that
world without us. Such a world would be without its lights
and darks, without its sounds and silences, and lacking both
the "things" we see and the "spaces" between that arise with

the seeing. We are, in fact, a "component" in a total configuration, a component that "decides" how the total configuration will *look*. We are a "figure" bringing our sensations to the whole gestalt, and thus "making sense" of a world that would be literal non-sense without us.

To be free is to rise up to the world, knowing that together we make a Whole and apart there is nothing. It is not that we *have* to do this. It is, rather, to realize that it is being done—that, in fact, we are all the time creating the world in our own perceiving and knowing and doing. From this vantage point we do not need to seek freedom but, rather, to realize it, since it has been ours all along. In the moment we give ourselves over to the momentary darkness of the now—without resistance, without strain, without effort, without expectation—we discover that this "darkness" is all we have, but out of IT we make all things.

7

Unchaining the Stars

IT WAS SAMUEL BUTLER who once noted that a hen is merely the egg's way of producing another egg. This backward way of putting things strikes most people as frivolous and therefore hardly a fruitful line of thought or inquiry. This derives from our notion that nature is basically stupid and that organisms which produce eggs operate according to "blind" instinct. Since an egg lacks even instinct, the suggestion that it may "know" how to make a hen seems absurd.

Genetically speaking, however, all living things have two distinct phases, the haploid and the diploid. We are most familiar with the diploid phase, the mature organism with a double (*diplo*) complement of genes. The haploid phase has a single (*haplo*) set of genes and is represented by an egg or, in the case of mammals, the sperm or ovum. Since the strongest drive of each phase is directed toward producing the other, the two phases constitute a single organic process. A living being might well be described as an alternation between the two phases, in which case hen-making eggs are as real as egg-making hens.

This implies that what things do is as important as what they are; indeed, that what things are *is* what they do. It is easy to denigrate the "body" as inferior to the "mind" until we remember that the body grows the mind—that "minding" is something the body does along with "skinning," "boning," "legging," and "arming." A body capable of growing an intelligent mind is an intelligent body, as is the environment that grew the body. A universe that is "treeing," "animaling," and "peopling" as well as "starring" and "planeting" is a universe to be watched—especially since it is the universe which has given rise to the watchers!

This way of looking at things implies that living beings are one of the more revealing things the universe does and that they might perhaps form a useful starting point for comprehending the rest. Nor has this point of view been entirely ignored. Forty years ago the philosopher Whitehead reacted against the materialist and positivistic reduction of nature to "a bloodless dance of categories" by speaking of "nature alive," [52] and constructing a powerful philosophy upon this idea.

More recently Teilhard de Chardin has developed a religious philosophy around the idea that life is the key reality, "that life is not a peculiar anomaly, sporadically flowering on matter—but an exaggeration, through favorable circumstances, of a *universal cosmic property*—that life is not an epiphenomenon, but the very essence of phenomenon." [53] Because of this "exaggeration" in living things, man is able to detect deep within himself an "interior" that must have "cosmic extension." This is to say that the existence of life in one part of the universe implies a "pre-life" throughout the universe, which Teilhard calls the "Within" of things.[54]

When we look at the whole universe we find that nothing so typifies it as its sheer creativity. Even the stars, which seem unchanged, are forever creating, slowly laying down the elemental foundations for everything else. In the center of most sunlike stars, hydrogen—the basic stuff of the universe—is slowly cooking into all the other ninety-odd elements. In smaller stars the process is very slow; in those much larger than our own sun it is a great deal more rapid. In our own sun, a typically average star, we are speaking of a cooking that is now about half done and will eventually last some eight or ten billion years. This is indeed a slow "burn," but it becomes more rapid toward the end, and may finally finish in a spectacular stellar explosion that will scatter its "ashes" throughout countless miles of space to make room for some new cosmic birth.

Condensed from hydrogen dust at its birth, a star is finally jettisoned back to dust at its death, but a dust much richer than before. Since this process has occurred uncountable times, especially by larger and faster stars than our own, the vast reaches of space are rich with all the elements known to man. Our own sun and solar system, late arrivals on the cosmic scene, are spun from the rich debris of stars that went before. The whole incredible process is like a giant version of the enrichment of topsoil—the continual breaking down of forests to give increased strength to trees to come.

The creativity of the stars is but a prelude to a story continuing without end—a drama with a smaller stage but with much more rapid action and perhaps more momentous results. In the coolness of vast interstellar spaces, on flying planets warmed by distant suns, the creative energy of geophysics and chemistry takes up where astrophysics ends. It is a long and complex story—of mountains forged and rivers carved, of a chemically rich sea turning into a living aquarium, of life adventuring into every tide bed and seashore, crawling onto the rocks and taking to the air—it is a spectacular tale with which we are more familiar, though the details are still being filled in.

It is true that we have no direct evidence that what has happened on earth has happened elsewhere. But everything we know about chemistry and physics, and everything we can surmise, impels us toward the conclusion that life is far from "accidental." It is part of the total designing, an expression of the same meandering creativity that built the elements in the stars and spun them into the intricate patterns of molecules and crystals and cells. Moreover, in a universe with an estimated ten billion galaxies containing a million million billion stars—with an inestimable number of spinning planets—the likelihood of life elsewhere is a virtual certainty.

Looking at the whole cosmic drift, then, we find a fundamental creativity stretching from atoms and elements in the stars all the way to the chemistry of planetary seawater, amino acids, proteins and protoplasm, and life itself—a creative adventure in which stellar debris gradually "comes to life," and later to consciousness, and finally to self-consciousness. Like hen-making eggs, ours is a life-making universe.

All this is done by the birth and death of the suns, by the creation and destruction of worlds. Nothing is fixed, nothing endures. We are so accustomed to thinking of creativity in terms of birth and life and the uphill road that we overlook the equally necessary decay and death, and the long downhill slide into dust and chaos. But creativity implies destruction, just as up implies down or light implies darkness. And if there is a meaning for "freedom" that makes sense in such a cosmos, it is the freedom all things show in letting go, in crumbling and breaking up to give room and life to the new. Nowhere is this more evident than in life itself, where nature has evolved as a transactional give-and-take—a mutual gobbling society in which living forms are slippery and always sliding down the gullet of something else.

The perpetual alternation of chaos/control, joy/sorrow, security/fear, pleasure/pain is, then, woven into the fabric of the universe—an endless yang-ing and yin-ning running through all things. If freedom is the acceptance of this flux, enslavement is the refusal to "let it roll." In the very act of clinging to *this* form, *this* structure, *this* role, *this* ego, *this* idea, *this* life, the onward *this/that* drift of things is dammed. Life immediately becomes a terrifying business, like trying to stand up in fast-running water.

This is not to imply that the whole universe is all flux and no form—or that it ought to be. It is, rather, to suggest that flux and form go together like *yang* and *yin,* and that pure flux without form is as meaningless as a painting that is all color with no shapes, or a piece of music that is one long note with no intervals. Likewise, pure form leads to evolutionary blind alleys—to creatures such as mastodons and dinosaurs, saber-toothed tigers and neanderthaloids—where rigidity of form prevents adaptation for survival. Yet even survival is not the criterion. Insects show superb adaptation, having evolved even the rudiments of social structure and colonization. But the external skeleton of the insects was a constriction from the start—a limitation in form that is conceivably all that prevented them from developing a larger size, and indeed control over the planet that instead passed to man.

Evolutionary success, then, has often depended on a kind of open or fluid structure, such as the internal skeleton of mammals, which allows for the differences between walking on four feet or on two, and between the evolution of paws or wings. Throughout his entire evolution man's development has maintained a balance by evolving forms that were flexible and open to change. Indeed, it was the "open" form of the anthropoid hand, neutral in a way that paws and claws are not, that allowed for the development of the opposable thumb and the toolmaking culture founded upon it. The overlay of cortical tissue on the human brain reflects the same openness to development, as does the more recent development of psychic "distance" upon which most of our social and psychological culture is built.

It is precisely here that our present danger lies: in the development of that psychic heredity known as culture. Culture consists primarily of "forms," or communally standardized ways of organizing reality—laws and language, institutions and roles. Such forms are the social "grids" that help us to organize and give "shape" to our social world by reducing it to a simpler pattern, in the same way that contour lines on a map allow us to grasp the "shape" of a landscape. Some of these cultural grids work extremely well, or work for a time and then fail to measure up to new social realities, in the same way perhaps that the tusks of the saber-toothed tiger failed to adapt. And if what we have been saying makes sense, it is worth asking whether perhaps the grids of our rational, "in here" world—the forms of our language and our thinking—have become too rigid and "closed" for adaptation in a world of constant and rapidly accelerating change.

The "in here" world of the intellect is made up of concepts constructed from the warp and woof of perception and language. But since our perceptions are interpreted primarily in the light of former concepts, the house of the intellect is virtually a house that language built. This is obvious to anyone who has done any thinking about thought, for all rational thinking is done in words. What is less obvious is that words represent "bits" of reality, and therefore their validity as measuring tools depends on there being a reality divisible in "bits." One could say, of course, that this depends on how you look at it—but looking leads back to interpreting what we see in terms of concepts! The result is a vicious circle.

Even less obvious is the fact that every language system embodies a whole set of basic assumptions that seem unquestionable. In the famous "Jabberwocky" poem, which Alice found in her Looking-Glass House, the following lines occur:

> 'Twas brillig, and the slithy toves
> Did gyre and gimble in the wabe;
> All mimsy were the borogoves,
> And the mome raths outgrabe.

"It seems very pretty," says Alice. "Somehow it seems to fill my head with ideas—only I don't know exactly what they are!"[55] But the *ideas* are obvious: that "toves" and "raths" are things, and that "gyring" and "gimbling" are something that "toves" (especially "slithy" ones) do. In other words, below the level of words and their dictionary meanings is an accepted set of grids having to do with a world supposedly made out of nouns (things), verbs (events), and adjectives (qualities).

This deep structure is apt to come through words that are virtually nonsense—convincing us that something meaningful is being said. Thus the Russian philosopher Nicolas Berdyaev once wrote that "history is the result of a deep interaction between eternity and time; it is the incessant eruption of eternity into time."[56] If this came from the mouth of the pope or the queen of England, it would possibly draw cheers, since it would be regarded as having "style" and "profundity." Yet virtually all that this statement has is real words in conventional order. Ponder "history," "eternity," "time," what it means for time and eternity to "interact," and what is meant by eternity "erupting" into time, and it becomes clear that abstractions are being strung together with only a pretense at dealing with the world "out there."

Beneath every such abstraction lies the deep structure of the noun, a real "thing" that can be moved about and can therefore function as the "subject" or "object" of a sentence. It was this deep structure which convinced philosophers that "goodness," "truth," and "beauty" exist "somewhere," and likewise still convinces people that there exists a "soul" which can survive death, and that the rock-hard foundation of their own identity is an "ego" somewhere inside. This became perhaps the most famous *error* ever noted by modern philosophy when Whitehead described it as the "fallacy of misplaced concreteness." [57]

It is still hardly realized that the "thinginess" of the noun is the cause of endless problems that countless philosophy undergraduates have debated into the night. Stuart Chase reports an example in his book *The Tyranny of Words*—a group of college students furiously arguing the question, "If there were no matter in space, would time go on?" But, as Chase points out:

Obviously there cannot be:

Something, somewhere, at no time   or
Something, nowhere, at some time   or
Nothing, somewhere, at some time.

Everything which happens must be structurally represented as something, somewhere, at some time. . . .

So far as we now know, this is the nature of every situation in the environment in which we live.[58]

But look how easily we become tied in such knots. "Does time have a beginning?"—an impossible question, since "beginning" makes sense only within time, not before it. "What if there were nothing rather than something?" —a pointless query, since the concept of "nothing" means *nothing* unless there is also "something." Or, "What was God doing before he made the world?"—a question that Augustine answered by saying, "He was preparing hell for those prying into such deep subjects." [59] The same tangle underlies the perennial question, "Do we live after death?" But "we" has meaning only within a span of time, specifically the "time" between birth and death. Beyond these points "we" ceases to refer to anything within time and space. Of course there is always someone to jump up with fire in his eyes and shout, "That's right! Because after death we then live *outside* time and space!" But once we are *outside* time and space, the concept "outside" ceases to mean anything, for insides and outsides can exist only within a world of space.

A friend, enrolled in a university course in science fiction, recently reported to me a class discussion about the future of intelligent beings. Once evolution develops creatures who are pure "mind" with no "bodies," what on earth will these creatures *do* with themselves? How will they occupy their time? This question apparently went round and round, becoming knottier by the minute. Finally my friend, who has a considerable knowledge of Hindu mythology, suggested that such beings would soon become bored with their tremendous mental skills. Like Brahma, the Hindu god of creation, who tires of his infinity and so sacrifices himself to the finite—becoming you and I—these very clever beings would probably invent some way to assume bodies again, if only to go out of their minds and come to their senses! As one might expect, this suggestion was ignored as being too easy, frivolous, or "mythical." As my friend put it, "They jumped right back into the knot!" [60]

This sort of debate is a modern version of the medieval debate about how many angels can dance on the head of a pin. The terms of the debate have not advanced an iota; they have simply changed. In place of "angels" we have switched to equally mythical abstractions such as "pure minds with no bodies," or pointless extrapolations such as "endless time," "infinite space," or "absolute nothingness." Equally bewitching to the modern mind are such conceptual end-alls as "The Unified Field Theory" and "Probability"—which are "scientific" versions of God and Fate.

The fact is that entities such as "mind," "soul," and "intelligence," or mysterious things such as "electrons," "atoms," and "organisms," are like those put-ons of old—"demons" and "monsters." They are thoughts about reality, which is to say they are reality gridded off into "things" according to current fashion. This is not to say that these things lack *any* meaning. Even demons and monsters have some "reality" about them. As one intelligent girl said to me one day, "If you had ever been haunted, you would believe that demons are very real!" [61] It is part of our scientific smugness that we deny demons while we assert the existence of such ghostly boogies as "complexes," "neuroses," "feelings," and "hang-ups." We still make everything into a "thing," though we now assert that our things are "scientific" rather than imaginary or mythical.

The problem with most of these scientific "things" is not that they are false, but that they are only half true. Nowhere is this more apparent than in the realm of living things where we habitually think of birds and animals as isolated and separate beings. The case is not so clear in the case of fish or trees, which obviously depend upon a particular environment. But we regularly think of ourselves as separable from our surroundings. This viewpoint seems to be verified by most of our activities. When we take aspirin we swallow only enough for the isolated organism—we do not ingest a whole bottle to patch up all our surroundings! But this is only half the story, for we may well have to swallow *more* aspirin in four hours, since the first dose has, in fact, been dissipated to the environment.

The fact is that we *are* connected, as the carefully designed ecosystems on spacecraft prove. We ignore this fact at our peril. It has now become apparent, for example, that there is no difference between poisoning the environment and poisoning people—only a time lag.

It would seem, then, that cultural grids, and particularly the grids of words and grammar, are "forms" as potentially constricting as overgrown tusks or heavy horns. Words provide us with a tyranny of in-*form*-ation, since it is information structured according to the arbitrary classes of the dictionary, unchanged for millennia. We are therefore hypnotized by our own word structures, which Bernard Gunther has so aptly called "Thing king."

> The problem of language:
> nouns and verbs.
> The actor
> separate from the action.
> I injured my finger
> rather than just hurting.
> Being the observer
> rather than the experience.
> There is no static aspect

of the self;
but thinking makes it seem so.
This hoax,
this commonly accepted fantasy
is a division
that starts the basic split;
within the mind ego
are all of the different aspects
of you; the good you,
the bad you,
the should you, the have you.
Endless talk, magic words
about reality
become realer than what is real,
until you are able to stop
and realize
you're only all
one self.[62]

"You're only all one self." But, as Ronald Laing has put it, "once the fissure into self and ego, inner and outer, good and bad occurs, all else is an infernal dance of false dualities." [63] The self in the guise of the ego's self-*concept* can only construct a universe out of shoddy pieces of conceptual time and conceptual space, ideas of what things are and ideals of how they ought to be. Such a false self is caught in the webs of in-*form*-ation and con-*form*-ity and thus forced to labor under the terrifying burden of an implacable universe.

It is obvious, then, that the grids of culture—the maps of social reality embodied in language, grammar, and our conceptual-symbolic ways of manipulating that reality—are forms as problematic for survival as the cumbersome size of the brontosaurus was for his. If this is obvious in terms of the natural environment—where we are busy "mastering" nature and "conquering" space—it is perhaps less obvious in the social environment. But, as Laing has suggested, the pattern of words leads us into treating people like "things" and the knotty logic of "us" and "them."

> Each person is the other to the others. The members of a scandal network may be unified by ideas to which no one will admit in his own person. Each person is thinking of what he thinks the other thinks. The other, in turn, thinks of what yet another thinks. Each person does not mind a colored lodger, but each person's neighbor does. Each person, however, is a neighbor of his neighbor. What They think is held with conviction. It is indubitable and it is incontestable. The scandal group is a series of others which each serial number repudiates in himself.[64]

It was the noun, of course, with its ability to provide a segmented reality of manageable "bits," that allowed for the development of science, since science depends upon the isolation of variables. But we are reminded that science leads to mechanical models for reality and mechanical means for manipulating it. Thus the fragmentation of society into "us" and "them" tends to set up a machinelike set of reactions, resulting in the feeling that the individual has lost control of the situation. Thus Laing continues:

> The peculiar thing about Them is that They are created only by each one of us repudiating his own identity. When we have installed Them in our hearts, we are only a plurality of solitudes in which what each person has in common is his allocation to the other of the necessity for his own actions. Each person, however, as other to the other, is the other's necessity. Each denies any internal bond with the others; each person claims his own inessentiality: "I just carried out my orders.

If I had not done so, someone else would have." . . . In this collection of reciprocal indifference, of reciprocal inessentiality and solitude, there appears to exist no freedom.[65]

In essence this is what leads men into the terrible machinery of what Charles Reich called the Corporate State, where man "does not run the machine; he *tends* it." [66] Where men have surrendered their identity, where no one thinks he is responsible but everyone else is ("They ought to do something about that!"), each person can rationalize his own dishonesty and corruption, his income-tax cheating, petty larceny, and secret lawlessness. When "everyone else" has a gun, having one yourself seems "right," even if illegal. The result is a kind of mutual-consent disorder in which society is perpetually on the brink of riot and revolution.

If this begins to sound like a pathological description, this is no accident. Laing's work on schizophrenia has shown that peculiar kinds of "splits" occur in people who confuse roles with reality, or who feel themselves to be a nonagent or a nonsubject at the disposal and mercy of outer circumstances. Such splits are only aggravated by the built-in capacity of technology for alarming rates of change. The helpless and fragmented ego experiences "future shock," which is largely the refusal of the world to meet the demands of stability and security required by the rational ego. His world begins to look like a "madhouse," and everyone seems to have "gone crazy." It is not surprising that a whole branch of modern literature and drama is devoted to portraying the insane and the absurd. Beckett's *Waiting for Godot*, Ginsberg's "Howl," Kerouac's *On the Road*, and the movie *Blow-Up* spring to mind.

It is symptomatic of our disease that we counter the rising tide of the absurd by clinging more desperately to what

small vestiges of rationality remain, failing to see that such
desperate clinging to reason is itself irrational. It was precisely our fear of madness, and the tyrannical demand for
reason, that propelled us toward the absurd in the first
place. For centuries now we have been bewitched by the intellect, by our so-called "rational" categories, by the belief
that conscious thought is supreme. Committed to building
civilizations upon predetermined ideologies, convinced that
instinct is "mere" instinct, that nature is "brute," and that
everything sensuous is a positive danger to our conscious
control, we have concocted a society where the only order is
founded on "law and order" and the only alternative to this
sterility is "revolution for the hell of it."

Any rational analysis of our present lack of freedom is
therefore a positive danger, since such analyses can only
convince us to apply "rational" solutions. We will therefore
be persuaded to try harder and exert more effort to solve
our problems. But all such efforts can only come to "knot,"
since they are founded on a corrupt notion of the self as a
separate intellect. The rational man is therefore incapable
of untangling his knots precisely because he is committed to
rational procedures that are bound to produce a tighter
knot.

This is apparent even in the midst of vast advances in
organization, mechanization, and computerization, which
only seem to produce more information on our problems.
Rational man has not been content to mingle reason with
feeling and imagination, but has become obsessed with
hammering and forcing reason to the hilt on every problem
—an obsession that has us compiling tons of data on everybody and everything, including photographs of the far side
of the moon and virtually every square yard of Asia. Eventually this leads to complex bureaucracies to oversee the

facts, information retrieval systems to find the facts, special studies to determine the facts, and complex methods of controlling those who have the facts to make sure they are not misused. This sort of fanatical regard for "The facts, Man! Nothing but the facts!" is a trap, for it leads to a vicious circle.

If there is a cure for our bondage to rationality, it must lie in an altogether different direction. It must lie beyond the grids of our conventional culture, which means beyond most forms of verbal description. This is to imply both that we *think* too much and that we *feel* too little—that we *think* of ourselves *as* (and think ourselves into *being*) divided from our surroundings rather than *feeling* that we are not. Confined to the conventions of language and culture, we are scarcely able to think of ourselves as anything but separate, since the conventional patterns of our thought are divisive and fragmenting. At the same time, we are desperately afraid of feeling, of all those ways of relating to our environment and to others that lie "below" conscious thought.

But surely it is obvious that consciousness itself is a sophisticated form of feeling. This is why so many of our "reasons" are really rationalizations, for we tend to develop or experience feelings first and then find reasons why these feelings are "right." Following this line of thought, it would seem that even our rational ways of controlling the so-called "irrational" or "unconscious" side of life are really rationalizations for what are basically irrational and subconscious feelings! There is simply no way, then, to apply "pure" reason to our problems, for even our ideas of purity derive from deeper feelings and instincts.

This way of looking at feeling may well irk those who have always regarded reason as supreme and feeling as dangerous and unreliable. But, in fact, the seat of conscious thought is the surface cortex of the brain, which is a relatively recent addition in the history of evolution. The conscious and intellectual side of man has derived from or emerged out of more fundamental unconscious or nonintellectual modes of awareness—which is what we mean by "feeling."

This suggests that the real *wisdom* of the organism that has allowed it to survive and adapt is the subcortical wisdom of feeling itself. This is not at all surprising, since it is feeling, for example, that makes us remove our hand from a hot stove rather than what we may happen to "think" about heat. Indeed, only after we have *felt* heat do we really know what to think about it! Thus it is the organism's ability to "feel" light waves through the retina, "feel" sound waves through the eardrums, and "feel" smells and tastes through the nose and tongue that allows it to adapt to environmental conditions without conscious "knowledge" of how it is done.

It was the genius of the philosopher Whitehead to grasp the importance of "feeling," not merely in terms of human experience but as an analogy for what goes on throughout the universe. Each entity, right down to the smallest electron, is a focal point for all the forces and influences of its particular "world." This means that the so-called "things" of the universe do not simply "confront" or "face" one another but, in fact, merge, transact, or blend. Just as each intersection of a net is influenced or "moved" by touching the net, each entity in the universe is "moved" by its connections with all the rest.

Whitehead described everything as "prehending" everything else, but the term "feeling" is easier to grasp. Thus we do not know how it "feels" to be an electron, an apple, or a tiger. To know how it feels, we would have to become the electron, apple, or tiger. But we do know how it "feels" to be a man. Taken as a whole, however, the universe is one immense creative discovery of "feeling" what it is like to *be* electrons and apples and tigers and men.

This is likely to disturb our ideas of what "things" are, but, as Charles Birch has put it, "we 'thingify' the electron and all other 'organisms' because we see them as static mechanisms, and not as perceiving entities." [67] To put this another way: if our *idea* of what things are is disturbed by the notion of them as "feeling" entities, it is only because ideas alone cannot capture the *depth* of things. What we need, then, is imagination, a reliance on intuition and the instinctual wisdom of our deeper selves—that is, less "thing king" and more feeling.

And so the unchaining of the stars is the unchaining of feeling itself. Out of the molten stellar furnaces come the cool waters and winds of the planets; out of the iron hardness of galactic rock emerges the resilient pliancy of living flesh; out of recalcitrant matter comes the responsive sensitivity of life. But the living things where this happens are not separate from the stars and rocks—they are the stars and rocks learning to "feel." What is increasing is the total "experience" of the universe in the sense that it has gradually discovered how to "feel" itself and, in man, to feel itself feeling itself.

Of course such an adventure is "dangerous," since whatever is soft and living and sensitive is also terribly vulnerable—capable of feeling pain and sorrow as well as pleasure and ecstasy and forced to endure death as well as life. So vulnerable is "feeling" that living things have evolved incredible ways to avoid it—like the bony shells of turtles or the armored skin of crocodiles. Man himself, a tenderskinned creature, has likewise developed protective devices against feeling. Alexander Lowen has spoken of "character armor," which is a use of muscular rigidity and tension in schizoids to reduce sensitivity.[68] But man's whole culture can be regarded as protective armor against undesirable sensitivity—the protective armor of clothes and city walls, shields and vaccines and tranquilizers, roles and masks and egos, "hard facts," "stable ideas," and a whole menagerie of abstract philosophies and religions to provide him with something permanent and certain in a universe of uncertainty and change.

The price of protecting ourselves, however, is the price of losing pleasure along with pain and sacrificing the ecstasy along with the sorrow. One can avoid the crushing despair of a broken love, but the only absolutely certain protection is to sacrifice the experience of love itself. But life persists and insists on "feeling" despite all attempts to avoid it, and wearing armor merely substitutes one kind of hardness for another. To fear death is to be afraid to live; to avoid danger is to be paralyzed by possibilities; to cling to stable ideas and philosophies of certainty is to lose the ability to respond to change and creativity.

There is, then, no way to stem the tide, for the stars will be unchained, just as water must flow. To resist the grand sweep of this adventure is to find oneself locked into a prison of fear and anxiety, like being chained to the oarlock on a sinking boat. But to give in is to find oneself on a "trip" that is literally the most "far out" trip there is, plunging minute by minute into that momentary darkness of the now out of which the whole adventure grows, like the sounds of a symphony out of the silence.

8

The Recovery
of Experience

WHAT DOES IT MEAN to understand something that happens—the movement of a star, for example? On the one hand, we find something in the world "out there"—a moving star. On the other hand, we have a set of concepts and models "in here"—mental concepts such as matter, energy, three-dimensional space and linear time. When we try to "understand" the motion of a star we arrange our "in here" constructs according to the rules of those constructs until we get a pattern that "fits" the "out there" motion of the star. If we have correctly understood the motion, we can extend the pattern through time and predict the motion or position of the star tomorrow or next year—a prediction that can then be verified by observation.

This is the procedure of science and the so-called empirical method of understanding the universe. The claim of this procedure is that it is based on direct observation and on observable "facts," which can be verified by anyone. It is "public" information. Science is therefore uninterested in concepts that cannot be verified by observation and testing, such as those "put-ons" of former times.

At least two things need to be said about these claims. In the first place, the idea that science is a collection of observable facts which anyone can verify for himself needs to be radically challenged. Science has moved into realms where most of its observations are of scales and dials reflecting as much the interests of the scientist as the reality he is observing. Moreover, even the observation of the dials and scales is no longer public. The equipment used in scientific laboratories—lasers, computers, electron microscopes, and holographic processing equipment—is not accessible to the common man; and most scientists can operate only those instruments which relate to their own specialty. The results of observations must be taken "on faith" even by other scientists.

It is one of those historical clichés that science overthrew medieval scholasticism and that men could now base their knowledge on direct observation rather than appealing to "authorities" such as Aristotle. (Poor Aristotle was always the villain in this cliché!) But as the geophysicist M. K. Hubbert has pointed out, there is a lamentable "reversion to authoritarianism" in science today "whereby statements, if made by proper 'authorities,' are to be accepted as valid" whereas "if a contrary statement is made by one who is not an 'authority' . . . little credence can be given to it." [69] Science has developed a new priesthood, a kind of brahman class whose "authority" derives from the sacred certification of the temple of learning—the university.

Rather than overthrowing ancient authorities and handing over the interpretation of life to the common man, science has substituted new authorities. These authorities seem even more necessary in our day, since the conceptual models and constructs are now beyond the comprehension of most people. The average man is therefore still very much out of touch with the real world in the sense that he believes science *is* in touch and he does not understand it!

In the second place, the idea that science understands the motion of a star by applying mental constructs to it also needs to be challenged. It is part of the new "authoritarianism" that science does give increased understanding. But once we have reduced the motion of a star to some kind of "orbit" with a particular "direction" and a specific "speed," what have we understood? We may be able to "predict"— and this is certainly one of the purposes of science. Moreover, in the case of a more down-to-earth example, such as the motion of gas particles subjected to heat, we may be able to utilize our findings for the purpose of "control." But being able to "predict" and "control" does not imply that we understand anything except how to manipulate our own symbols.

The fact is that we *understand* almost nothing about the universe in which we live. The illusion that we do is the illusion of our own concepts and purposes imposed on nature. For what, after all, is the motion of *a* star—of *any* star, of *all* the stars—but so much sublime nonsense? We fail to see it this way, of course, mainly because our conceptual systems delude us into taking it all as a deadly serious business.

But when we think about all those mountains and hills, flowers and trees, fish and birds and animals—what a funny business all this is! And when we think of all our Lilliputian conquests and wars, political ploys and economic crashes— what a funny business this is too. At this point a bit of resistance sets in, especially among those politicians, bankers, and businessmen who have a vested interest in taking it all seriously. But this does not alter the fact that what goes on under the dubious rubric of "civilization" is mostly sublime nonsense or exalted monkey business—which amounts to roughly the same thing!

Immediately the cries go up in all directions: that human

life *does* have *meaning* and *purpose*. Moreover, all those
seemingly pointless plants and animals have a purpose since
we eat them, and even the stars produce a planetary home
for *us*. This logic is based on the old notion of nature as a
hierarchy with man at the top. But once we see that the
whole of nature is an ecosystem, this logic collapses as nonsense. Otherwise we are forced into saying that *we* have a
purpose because we provide food for maggots and rats!

Again, responses are predictable. If we do not have some
innate purpose, then we have to *create* one: we have to
"live" responsibly and do "meaningful" work, "contribute"
something to society and "further" human knowledge. But
is the purpose of life to live, and go on living until we die?
Is it to stave off death by reproducing ourselves, thus passing off the question to our children? Is it to live and work
amid the fury of freeways and suburbs, working to keep the
freeways and suburbs going, buying appliances on time, and
having the security of an insurance payoff at death? Is it to
struggle to wipe out poverty and racism and warfare, to im-
prove society and work toward global democracy, continually cutting heads off a monster that keeps growing new
ones until one of the heads sneaks up behind and gobbles us
up? Is it to pursue knowledge to the moon, and thence to
the stars, only to break our skulls against the imponderables
of time and space, and finally to gnash our teeth in despair
at gaps we can never cross?

Or is the meaning of life found in forgoing such nonsense? Is it perhaps to be free of all this, refusing both the
commercial sops and competitive blows thrown at the poor
little ego? Is it perhaps to repudiate the whole ego show—
along with the political games, ideological nonsense, and
the technological stupidity that breeds the poverty and the
racism and the warfare? And if *this* is it, where in fact will

this get us? But surely it is clear that this too will get us no-where, and that getting "somewhere" is based on the dubi-ous assumption that life does have meaning.

But if life is, in fact, meaningless, what are we to make of *that?* The fact is that we can make anything of it we want, for if life *did* have meaning, it would hardly be worth living. After all, when we really begin to think it through, all our tasks and projects, all those frantic jobs we do with their al-leged "purposes" and "goals," are aimed at what comes after hours—music and painting, dancing and singing and lovemaking, vacationing or traveling, or just "goofing off." But what is the purpose of painting a landscape? Is it to color the canvas? Is the purpose of playing music to get to the end? Is the point of dancing to move around the floor? Is lovemaking simply to bear children? Is goofing off a meaningful activity?

"Of course it is!" says the pragmatist, who thinks that art and music are "therapeutic," that we vacation to "relax," or travel to "get away from it all." This is the disease of the Protestant ethic and Puritan earnestness—believing with a passion that work has meaning, which leads to sophisticated rationalizations for not working. This kind of thinking leads to the absurdity that we play so that we can work harder, that food is strictly a source of nutriments to keep us alive, that the world full of all this myriad of colors and sounds and smells is simply there to give "food for thought," and that the whole point of life is to tighten up our mental cate-gories and disciplines for the next generation.

Such thinking leads to the notion that stars do, in fact, have a meaning, even if it is just a little beyond our under-standing; and that spiders and lizards and daffodils and tumbleweed are primarily grist for our science "courses" (courses to where?)—data to fill out our classification schemes so that they are eventually "complete." By this ruthless procedure all the joyous nonsense of our marvelous world is hammered, forced, and divided into academic "disciplines" which are then force-fed to youth as part of a "meaningful" and "relevant" education.

If by now my own views on all this are not evident, let me summarize them this way: at the risk of offending most of our glorious institutions—libraries, churches, universities, governments, and other stately monuments to our allegedly "purposeful" lives—I assert that all of this is so much intellectual crap. The problem is that most of our intellectuals lack what Ernest Hemingway called "a built-in, shock proof crap detector." [70]

Let me suggest that all those stars are going around to entertain each other, that octopuses and electric eels are staging a show called "I can scare you more than you can scare me," that giraffes are finding out what it's like to have a tremendously long neck, that a tumbleweed is discovering what it's like to have no place to go and lots of time to get there. In this vein, a dancer is finding out what it's like to move to music, a spaceman is discovering what it's like to walk on the moon, and an uptight businessman is finding out how this feels when you take it all seriously.

It should be apparent by now that any statement of purpose or meaning is fishy, or downright funny—like a baboon with a worried look on its face. Perhaps all such purposes look like non-sense, precisely because purposes are what we concoct in our heads. If so, perhaps we ought to do less thinking about all this and explore a little how it all feels.

Thus if we think about all those after-hours activities that work seems directed toward, we find that music is as central to life as anything—forming an integral part of radio programming, television commercials, movie sound tracks, stereo recording, religious worship, public ceremonials, marriages, deaths, and nine tenths of all nightclub entertainment. Now music, of all the arts, can hardly be said to have "meaning." Indeed, nothing spoils music more than to have to "get something out of it."

Many people think that music must have meaning, but this is largely a hangover from the nineteenth century, when everyone was so addicted to the idea of a progressive civilization that composers concocted "program" music. Thus works such as Beethoven's *Sixth Symphony* (*Pastorale,* 1808), Berlioz' *Symphonie Fantastique* (1830), Tchaikovsky's *Symphonie Pathétique* (1893), Richard Strauss's *Also sprach Zarathustra* (1896), and Stravinsky's *Le Sacre du Printemps* (1913) were written with definite "stories" in mind or with well-defined philosophies to express. These stories are now written on record jackets, leading people to think that they don't "understand" music unless they know what it *means*—that is to say, unless they have an explanation of what all the brass in the third movement was "for."

But when we turn back to the purely instrumental music of the baroque period in the seventeenth and eighteenth centuries—the works of Handel and Vivaldi and Bach, for example—or when we turn to specifically instrumental forms of twentieth-century music, like some forms of blues, jazz, and rock, we discover a delight in sound itself—in the intermingling of melody and harmony for its own sake, in the solo flight of a harp or organ, drums, piano, flute, or guitar, without any attempt to "say" anything. To claim meaning for such delightful nonsense is to imply that tones and chords are somehow incomplete in themselves.

The whole notion of *meaning* derives from our view of

man as primarily a thinking creature, deriving thoughts from things or making things conform to thoughts. Thinking is thing-ing, which is to say that it is a visually oriented activity aimed at developing and manipulating images of permanence. "Meanings" are firm, conscious, and capable of being expressed in words, and they derive directly from the idea of language as an "in here" set of meanings referring to the "out there" world.

But music crashes all this to the ground, since it appeals directly to man as a feeling creature. Feeling is not tied to things; it is not static, material, or permanent, and therefore does not require any meaning beyond itself. Music, therefore, does what no thought can do: it provides us with a living experience of the present moment—the now which has no meaning beyond itself because it is "complete." Since music contains all meanings within it, there is no meaning that can possibly be added to it. As Victor Zuckerkandl puts it, music gives us "images in which there is nothing to be seen, spaceless *Gestalten*, constructions in which everything flows. . . . The new dimension by which music enriches our image world . . . is *time,* and everything for which the word stands: flowing, becoming, change, motion." [71] In the midst of music, meaning coalesces with experience.

But, with a little imagination, the whole universe begins to look like a grand orchestration, with billions of stars going "pling, pling" in the darkness, with supernovas now and then going "boom!" as they explode, with mountains and valleys going up and down like musical rhythms, and with comets and swordfish and dolphins and delphiniums and people—each doing his own solo flight in the midst of tremendous orchestrated accompaniment. And so we say,

"Look here. . . . Now see here! . . . Listen to me!" as if to say, "Watch how *I* play this thing!"

It is not accidental that music is the universal art form. Since it lacks the cultural grids of language and thought, it can be appreciated by anyone without being "translated." Indeed, translation is impossible between various musical structures, our own and the very different harmonic structures of certain Eastern music; but this is an insignificant barrier which is easily bridged, precisely because the imagination can grasp new structures if there is no meaning barrier. More important than this, however, is the fact that music somehow duplicates or images reality as a whole: the fundamental light/dark, up/down, in/out, life/death rhythms of existence. We beat our hearts and breathe, we wake and we sleep, we live and we die—and the sounding and silencing of musical notes seems to capture this directly.

It has been noted that precivilized man lived primarily in an auditory world—in jungles alive with the sounds of nature, in a culture where the spoken word was a thing of majesty and magic. Civilized man, however, has moved into a visual world of colors and shapes, which is un-sound in both senses of the word. Seeing is the most aloof of our senses, largely because it is possible "at a distance," and this aloofness has been incorporated into our whole civilization. Our culture is an eye culture. We urge others to "see for yourself" and we claim that "seeing is believing." Great men of intuition and wisdom are reduced to being "visionaries" with "in-sight." The sense of sight has been exalted at the expense of the rest.

Most of the abstractions in modern urban life are based primarily on the sense of sight, on cleverly calculated curves and angles. We have come to accept the huge skyscraper and the "well laid out" green belt as beautiful, even though we are forced to look at them to the accompaniment of unbearable noise from traffic and repulsive smells from factories. Emphasizing only part of the sensorium, we have constructed a fragmented environment consisting mainly of highly visible ego-extensions. It is promoted and sold to us in the same fragmented way: by sexuality—a fundamentally tactile experience!—reduced to a visual television image of a beautiful woman in one or another state of undress, a total stranger who is simultaneously seen by twenty million viewers.

While we are thus bombarded by visual images and abstract ideas, we are victims of tactile deprivation. Our educational system, founded upon symbolic manipulation (reading, writing, arithmetic), is notably lacking in any real encounter with tangible things. This deprivation has its effects which are nowhere so apparent as in the usual pattern of sexual development in adolescents.

As has been discovered in recent psychological research,[72] most children first encounter sexual behavior visually—through the media and, more often than we generally suspect, the sexual exhibitionism of older adolescents or relatives. Their sexual feelings are formed primarily through *ideas:* the early encounter with "dirty" words or quite unimaginable descriptions of parental intercourse presented by older children—descriptions almost universally frightening or shocking to a child. All of this is reinforced by further *ideas* from parents, usually along the lines that sexual experimentation is dangerous, debilitating, and corrupt.

It has been widely accepted today—though not usually emphasized for fear of disturbing parents—that one of the major functions of the modern college campus is to provide an "open" atmosphere for sexual experimentation, development, and maturity. This is a highly important function, considering the state of sex education in our schools. Most college students report that their first sexual encounter was approached as a relatively traumatic experience, largely because of the accidental miseducation in their earlier years. Yet recently it has been realized, and verified by hundreds of college students, that these sexual encounters during the premarital years turn out to be a form of "therapy" that, most of the time, undoes most of the damage.

This suggests that the education of the mind and the dissociated visual sense alone is inadequate for the development of wholeness and personal identity. We are creatures who are deeply rooted in a tactile encounter with others throughout development. Ignoring this can only lead to nervous disorder, psychic splitting, and identity breakdown. Yet we continue to exalt the brain and denigrate the body, scorning all forms of sensitivity training, and acting as if touching is childish, crude, "sexy," and definitely not something to be done in public.

But if the sense of touch is primary, if feeling is the very touchstone of our connections with reality, then it is obvious that we need to recover not only a sense of feeling but a depth of feeling if we are to be whole organisms. What this includes is of course the breakdown of the "out there"/"in here" split which the sense of sight encourages, and the development of "out there"/"in here" unity which touch and the other senses promote.

The problem is that as soon as we move from visual to tactile encounters, we feel insecure. We know how to deal with the most alluring sights without giving ourselves away, for we can stay aloof and "keep a straight face." But we are not so adept at dealing with other alluring sensations—

sound, for example. Sound soon begins to "take over," we "lose control," and shortly we find ourselves jiggling knees, stamping feet, clapping hands, and bobbing heads. What will people think?

Even more frightening is the prospect of opening ourselves up to those feelings which are emotional, since we suddenly find ourselves confronting that seething, wormy world of our deeper selves, full of all those broken and ruined parts of ourselves which we have been repressing all along. Suddenly we are face to face with the dark side of the universe: the indelible past come back to haunt us; the pitchy darkness of the future looming ahead. We sense the movement within of ugly forces long-repressed, germinating in the unconscious like bulbs in a black cellar. We catch the dim outlines of some dark creature—the Devil, or Evil, or our own Original Sin, or Death . . . Nothingness. The more we follow the dark trails of this "insearch," the worse the landscape becomes. James Hillman has described it as follows:

> The beast emerges from his lair where he has long lain sleeping, and a man has night terrors, awakens in a sweat. A corpse or ancestral mummy resurrects. A vast swamp appears behind the Church or behind one's father's house, from which crawls a prehistoric monster with an elongated red phallic neck. . . . A criminal, an idiot child, a piece of feces inside the water spigot staining the fresh water as it flows. . . .
>
> At these moments, when one meets face to face the perverse and amoral creatures who have been inhabiting other parts of the building . . . one squirms having to acknowledge the dark truth about oneself.[73]

It is clear why all this has been repressed. It is *yin* rather than *yang*, darkness rather than light, feeling rather than

thought, chaos rather than order. It is slippery and dangerous, insecure and frightening, messy, vulgar, and above all
incomprehensible. Better to live in the clear light of the rational, better to ride the crests and pretend the troughs are
not really there. Better to keep all this terrible chaotic jum-
ble in the cellar.

But *who* is going to be the keeper? The intellect? How do
we know its motives are pure? If the intellect is only the
upper side of feeling, in what sense does it control the under
side? Does the head side of a coin control the way the tail
side will fall? Does the bright side of the moon direct the
dark side? Does the ego control the id? Or is the ego/id
really some kind of *yang/yin* unity: egoid, ei-god, go-die,
ideog, digeo?

But then it becomes clear that there is nothing to do but
live with the irrational, to tolerate the creeps and monsters,
and to realize that these are only the underside of ourselves.
This has been the everlasting theme of literature since literature began—of Odysseus in the cave of Cyclops, of Daniel
in the lions' den and Jesus in the wilderness with Satan, of
Beowulf stalking Grendel's mother under the sea, of
Dante's journey over the frozen hulk of Satan to reach the
gate of heaven, of the Red Cross Knight in the Den of Error
and Lear on the heath, and of Frodo the hobbit who has to
pass through the gloomy lair of the spiderlike Shelob before
he can complete his mission.

Life itself is founded upon these monsters and creeps, as
Oriental statues of gods standing upon demons and gremlins would suggest.[74] We are particularly haunted by such
uglies which we feel compelled to flush down the toilet,
burn, bury, or bulldoze out of sight. Yet they keep popping
up in the very midst of life itself, so close as to wrench and
chill. Confronted with pictures of open-heart surgery or

human birth, enlargements of our own spermatozoa and antibodies, or an electron microscope photo of our own neurons, we are again reminded that the world of living things is mostly a twisted, globular, weblike, snaky-looking mass of slimy tangled "beasts" as frightening and mysterious as Grendel of old.

It is, of course, precisely this tangled mass of fear and mystery that gives rise to imaginative art and the farther reaches of inspired creativity. For far down in the tangle, among the mythical beasts, Freudian symbols, and Jungian archetypes, lie the engraved experiences of the past, burning with a terrifying energy. But the imaginative artist—the Raphael or Blake or Berlioz, Basho, Tagore, or Picasso—is precisely that man who has taken the risk of plunging into the tides of his own subrational depths, who has penetrated hell in order to rise to heaven.

The conventional wisdom of ordered society is largely opposed to the imaginative exploration of feeling, precisely because it unlocks the doors of heaven and hell. Mystics and prophets have never been popular. Thus, while the creative imagination ranges through a vertical dimension of heights and depths, most institutional forms of government, education, and religion tend to remain within a horizontal plane of reason and order—which is to say, very much "on the level." Feeling and imaginative exploration is highly suspect, since it challenges the established values of a rational society. But it is precisely in this exploration that the imaginative artist restores wholeness and freedom, not only within himself but also within society. For in tapping the energy of his own mysterious "depths" and the inspiration of his own imaginative "heights," he synthesizes and joins and re-creates the world in what Blake called a "marriage of heaven and hell."

To resist imagination and feeling, to resist the irrational upheavals of the unconscious, is to pursue the myth of the ego—suggesting that we can in fact stand apart from *yin* in the pure rational whiteness of *yang*. Paradoxically, this only leads to more vulnerability, since the separate ego immediately feels overwhelmed, not only by the hidden side of the physical organism but also by the deep-flowing tides of the whole universe. The ego thus finds itself right back in the trap of isolated consciousness, rattling around in a hostile galaxy with only a trembling handhold separating it from blackness and death.

Such resistance, however, only intensifies the fear and hardens the organism. Sensitivity unleashes too much that is frightening, for which reason the ego approaches life with the injunction, "Beware, beware!" instead of the willingness to be aware.

But once the ego is experienced as an illusion, as a fiction drummed up for the purpose of social survival but not particularly valuable in the cosmos as a whole, a new mode of feeling is opened up. Once we understand that there is no separate organism but only a single organism/environment field, it is obvious that the seething monsters are not particularly one's own responsibility. All the rage and upheaval of the unconscious is something the whole universe is doing, just as the whole universe is doing YOU at a particular time and place. Thus, in the midst of feeling the YOUniverse, there ceases to be anything to be afraid of. We can give ourselves up to feeling and emotion, to the tremendous tides of all those repressed guilts and fears and hang-ups, knowing full well that they are simply the minor chords of the symphony upon which the major melody of happiness is woven.

In a universe that is whole, there is simply no place to escape to, and all such isolated "places" are the *maya* of too much thing-think. We are here; the whole universe is here; and both the heights and the depths are here. All things are fused at the center.

Freedom, then, is not found by some kind of philosophical escape route, like a secret passage out of a dungeon. Freedom consists, rather, in realizing that the dungeon does not exist or is of our own making, a prison formed by seeing our-selves as encased and trapped in a shell apart from the rest of our surroundings. But in a uni-verse that is whole, all such prison walls are illusory, and all fear caused by what we imagine on the other side of the walls is likewise illusory. There is, of course, a danger in this—a danger that the conservative mind sees with impressive clarity, particularly since its interest is in conserving what order now exists. According to this line of thought, we must maintain the illusion that feeling and emotion are dangerous, evil, and corrupting; otherwise societal order will rapidly break down. Once we let the cat out of the bag, so this argument goes, all hell will break loose. If there are no restraints on the darker impulses of man, it is but a small step into the degrading practices of prostitution, drinking, gambling, and unrestrained pleasure-seeking. Everyone might well decide to become a "dropout," in which case mankind would lapse back into the savagery of primitivism. The only thing that keeps people in rational control of themselves is the fear of humiliation, ostracism, and punishment imposed on uncontrolled hedonism by a rational and ordered society.

In all fairness it must be admitted that this is a possible result of the unrestrained pursuit of feeling; and it is easy to produce our own examples to prove the point. Even to claim that sensuous feeling is as important as rational thought is to unleash Dionysian possibilities—particularly the possibility of a society devoted to the "free" expression of their repressed desires—and hatreds. The result of this variety of freedom is conceivably a culture which is one long drunken, stoned, orgiastic, sado-masochistic, orgasmic, rock-festival-like frenetic stupor!

But the recovery of feeling and experience does not have to mean anything of the sort. To pursue freedom by an uncontrolled reversion to sensuality is to become as completely enslaved as someone who pursues "rational" freedom through such paths as Christian salvation, Buddhist *nirvana,* Marxist dialectics, positive-thought Pealism, Republican party politics, Hare Krishna cultism, astrology, Zen, free enterprise, macrobiotic cooking, trade unionism, back-to-naturism, or Consciousness Three. Freedom is not found along any path—rational, cultic, or sensual—but is, rather, freedom from all such paths.

The point is that pursuing sensuality to achieve freedom leads directly to such enslaving feelings as guilt or boredom. This in turn leads to a frantic attempt to pursue pleasure faster, either to whitewash the boredom or to accumulate finally so much pleasure that one can retire, like a rich prostitute. This, of course, never quite works out. It has the same self-defeating effect as feeling so guilty and bored with being at war that one throws more and more bombs at the poor enemy, until one is so completely enslaved to bomb-throwing that one cannot stop.

This is not to suggest that we ought to feel so uptight about sensuality that we "restrain ourselves" completely, repressing the temptations of cigarettes, liquor, grass, premarital and extramarital sex, pornographic movies, fellatio, cunnilingus, mate-swapping, group orgies, and the rest. If freedom is seen as restraining oneself from everything, then one is once more enslaved to an idea of freedom. But once it is realized that doing these things is not the way to freedom, and that *not* doing them is likewise not the way to freedom, one is free to do them without, however, being hung up about them. The fact is that if done in and for themselves, rather than as a means to something else, there is nothing wrong with the wildest far-out sexual acrobatics. If they happen, they happen. To avoid them at all costs is to become as maniacal as someone who pursues six orgasms a day.

The final argument against this approach to life usually runs as follows: Suppose everyone was this free—wouldn't things become rather messy and chaotic? This was the point made by John Kenneth Galbraith in his review of Reich's *The Greening of America*: If everyone becomes a dropout, who will mind the store? [75]

But it is a reasonably certain guess that *everyone* will never be this free, any more than everyone will ever be a Christian, a Marxist, or a vegetarian. It is virtually certain that numerous people will continue to be totally tangled and boxed in by their own ideals and ideologies, platforms, creeds, abstractions, and symbolic ego-extensions. If societal "order" somehow depends upon such entanglements, we can probably assume that societal order will remain, even while society runs wild with rebels crying, "Wolf!"

From quite another point of view, freedom without the contrast of order is quite incomprehensible, like pure flux without any structure. The real danger is in a total enslavement to ideas by an entire civilization, or in total freedom from ideas by everyone, as Reich seems to advocate. But it is clear that freedom exists as itself part of a harmony and balance. The escape to freedom is therefore not a total repudiation and it does not require a "revolution." It is, rather, a subtle shifting of the center of gravity, a movement from being tangled in cultural ideas to being less so.

The recovery of experience and feeling is therefore not the *only* possibility—which is what a "revolutionary" philosophy would maintain. Such a recovery would only be a worse tyranny than the condition it replaced. It is, rather, an alternative, a way of living that many people will inevitably reject, while others accept it without question.

Thus when I go out and lie in the sun on the grass, listening to the sound of wind in the trees, something happens that is almost impossible to explain. There are two kinds of space: the space of "there," which is a perpetual problem for my mind, and the space of "here," which is pure experience. When I *think* about the time of "there," I cannot comprehend its infinity, nor grasp its "dimensions," nor even understand why it is "there" at all. But when I try to think about "here," all such intellectual problems disappear. The "here" is so close that it completely eludes and subverts thought, just as one's head eludes all efforts to see it. At the same time I experience no problem of *why* it is "here": I simply experience. And in experience everything is "here."

In the same way, the only time I can *think* about is time "then"—the then of past and future which I can "locate" along a construct like a time line. But if I think about time "then" too long, I get into incredible knots—about how it began and how it will end, where it is coming from and where it is going. On the other hand, when I try to think about the other kind of time—time "now"—I discover that it too eludes me. I cannot even speak it, for as soon as I say "now" I have merely labeled a moment that has already slipped away. At the same time, the "now" of my experience somehow includes every time.

And when I try to think about all of It, the whole universe, I find I can think about myriads of "things" and "events" in the world "out there." But as soon as I try to think the thinker of all this—as soon as I try to "eye" the "I" behind it all—I find that I can find nothing at all. "I" turn out to be a complete void, a hole in the middle of the whole cosmos in which that wholeness seems to reside. I am therefore aware of a most amazing paradox: that "I" *am* an immense darkness which seems to hide right behind my eyes, leaving me with "nothing to fall back on," and yet that all those stars and galaxies are shining in the midst of that void which is me.

It begins to dawn on me that my old ego-bound way of looking at things was not only, as Alexander Lowen puts it, a "betrayal of the body," but a betrayal of the whole universe—for it is "I" sparkling the outermost stars and sounding out the whole orchestration. Grasping at the ego is somehow to obscure all this, since it imposes a dichotomy on the void that is not there. And I realize that freedom is precisely that "voidness"—that clarity which comes not from clear ideas but from no ideas at all. But it is precisely that void which makes all things possible, as Lao-tzu put it centuries ago:

> The Way is a void,
> Used but never filled:
> An abyss it is,
> Like an ancestor
> From which all things come.[76]

Like a mirror that is clean and clear, the void called "I" can "reflect" all things. Like the pure white light of the sun, it can "color" all things; like the absolute silence of empty space, it can "sound" a whole symphony. To try to know myself is therefore as pointless as trying to reflect a mirror or hear silence. The point of that inner void is that it is "pointless" and can therefore entertain all possible points and shapes, colors and sounds. Without any point at all, it is like the invisible center of a circle, but it is a center around which the universe revolves.

Thus the sky circles over my head like a dome and the horizon circles me where the circle of the sky meets the circle of the earth. The "eye" with which I see all this is the whole universe "eyeing" itself, bringing the world into focus, "getting IT all together," looking at IT-self and seeing how IT-ALL looks. In the midst of this vast void, at the center of all those immense and meaningless galaxies orchestrating out there in those black immensities, I suddenly realize that it is the bewildering and incomprehensible meaninglessness of all this music that makes the whole thing worth living. But that is a rather late discovery, and not particularly original with "me." That the "whole thing" has always been "worth living" is precisely why "I" am "here" in this moment called "now" making the discovery.

9
The Only Freedom

THE WORST TYRANNY is not the one imposed by a dictator, nor is the worst prison a jail. We are only truly imprisoned by the tyranny of our own ideas, abstractions, and absolutes. It is easy, as Krishnamurti has often said, to escape from outer authorities but very difficult to escape from inner authorities. Nor are these simply those inner beliefs by which we direct our lives—such as religious or moral ideas —but rather those more fundamental assumptions on which these are built.

In Western civilization the most insidious such assumption is that we are each primarily a separate, rational intellect. This fundamental fallacy of isolation blinds us to the truth that most of the crises around us really derive from within—from the ego estranged from its world. The crisis of identity is therefore the central one and the key to all the rest.

The failure of modern man is the failure to see and feel himself as a complete organism enmeshed in an organism/ environment field. Instead, he sees himself as a mind trapped in a vulnerable body and a hostile world. This illusion leads to conflict, confrontation, and conquest as the dominant modes of action and behavior. Centuries of this approach to nature are now rebounding in our faces as the poison seeps back into our own blood and bones. If man brings on some kind of ecocatastrophe, his demise will simply be part of the total adjustment of nature, weeding out extremes in the interests of harmony and balance.

Apart from being a positive danger to everyone, the isolated ego is particularly vulnerable. It needs to be patted and praised, continually reinforced, boosted, and put on a pedestal. It demands prestige, status, authority, and power. It is not equipped to accept a humble place in the universe —unless it can somehow turn humility into heroism. It is therefore ripe for suffering and for exploitation.

The real organism requires only food, clothing, shelter, and a satisfactory sex life, and, perhaps, a few nonmaterial "goods" such as laughter, communication, and a bit of dancing. With this alone, man can rise to the heights of creativity, as Aurignacian man was proving in Altamira Caverns in France ten thousand years before the urban revolution. But the illusory ego requires tons of extra trash— closets and drawers full of clothes and shoes, jewelry, makeup, mechanical gadgetry, electronic apparatus, flashy cars, and paper ego-boosters such as diplomas and degrees. Moreover, the isolated ego requires a steady stream of this stuff so that it can keep up with all the other isolated egos.

None of this abstract and shiny junk is sold to the real, whole, human being but rather to the abstract self—which is lost in the mazes of commercial sex, status symbols, paper securities, and hidden persuaders. It is sold to frightened people who can combat their fears only by various forms of ego-tripping, or by the illusory game of building an environment that is largely made of ego-extensions. And it is sold on false promises, since no amount of "prestige," "status," and "power" can satisfy the insatiable ego.

Part of this ego-game are the clubs, societies, and institutions that pretend to treat people as non-egos by meeting and sharing together. But most of these groups—Masons, Shriners, Catholics, Mormons, Knights of Columbus, S.C.M. and S.D.S., Daughters of the American Revolution, Birchers, the P.E.O. Sisterhood, Klanners, Panthers, Communists, and Women's Liberation—simply form Group Egos. Under the guise of the Righteous Cause these groups reward those who make donations by granting in-group status while putting the rest into an inferior out-group. Every Group Ego, religious or political or racial or whatever, simply ends up playing the selfish game of We-are-less-selfish-than-You.

And finally, there are the really Big Egos: the governments of the major "powers." They too are abstract and are addicted to "saving face." Appealing to people who believe in abstractions, they are able to "sell" themselves with abstract nonsense like "honor" (An honorable peace!), "victory" (We shall not be humiliated!), and "power" (This great nation of ours!). Having grown up and therefore rejected such childish practices as carrying off the wives of the enemy, the Big Egos now make war against such abstract enemies as "communism" or "totalitarianism" —and justify it by such abstract metaphors as the "domino theory" or the protection of one's "sphere of influence." But ultimately the Big Ego is indomitable, and will destroy everyone else in "retaliation" rather than suffer defeat.

Nowhere does such abstraction reach such absurd heights as in the realm of economics, which is now largely a matter of shuffling paper.[77] We are caught in the conceptual bind that in order to survive people must possess paper money rather than food. Therefore everyone must work for money,

even if there is more than enough food to go around. Thus
the poor starve and the excess food rots!

The payoff for our incredible technological advances
ought to be a release from work. But we are caught in the
double bind of a conceptual work ethic and an abstract
paper economy which cannot allow for freedom from
work. Our technologists are therefore put to work on abstract tasks such as photographing Mars or designing a foolproof defense system.

One might argue that in a world of fools something must
be foolproof. But so enslaved to concepts are we that we
cannot even *see* a few simple realities of our situation. So
enslaved are we to the symbolism of money that we cannot
feed the hungry without imposing the humiliation of "welfare" or "charity." So enamored are we to numbers that we
get in a panic over reduced "production" even though we
are already loaded down with more things than we can possibly use. So confused are we between money and food that
we believe there will be food as long as we have dollars to
buy it—even though we now have DDT in our fat from
efforts to raise productivity in the farms and orchards of
America. So bewitched are we by numbers and totals and
skyrocketing graphs that we believe America is the "rich-
est" nation in the world because we have the highest Gross
National Product—even though our "wealth" includes
more and more poisoned air, polluted water, depleted
mines, and ruined landscapes every day.

What all this shows is that we confuse ideas and abstractions *about* things with things themselves. We confuse the
ego with the larger self, money with wealth, and figures with
facts—just as we have always confused words with things
and symbols *for* reality with *reality itself*. We are not con-

tent simply to live but have to "justify our existence"; we are not content with a balance of power but have to establish military "superiority." For such is the tangle of the abstract: having limited ourselves to the woefully vulnerable little ego, we are forced to overcompensate by "proving" in every way, again and again, that we are not really vulnerable at all.

Our confusion nowhere becomes so problematic as when we get embroiled in debates over "what to do about it." Here pacifists and activists, Christians, Marxists, liberals, and guerrillas join hands in a dance of idiocy. The idea that "we" can "do" anything is based on the separation of the ego from its problem—when, in fact, the separation *is* the problem. Every solution to what we ought to do is therefore contaminated by assumptions that make a solution impossible. Even the reverse—that "we" ought to "do" nothing—is equally contaminated.

The fact is that our whole concept of action is based upon bad assumptions. Revolution as a deliberate product of conscious purpose is therefore a fiction. We believe that "freedom" is a state that can be attained through some definite course of action, but in a universe that is a total field of interrelated processes, the isolation of a controllable course of action is purely conceptual. Moreover, a course of action can lead to freedom only if the course of action itself is free—in which case we are already acting freely and have nothing to achieve! This is the fallacy of coercing people to revolt. If this is not grasped, then the pursuit of freedom becomes a form of slavery, since we are *compelling* ourselves to actions that will be free only if they are spontaneous. It would seem, then, that there is little likelihood of freedom for anyone who maintains the usual ideas on how to get it.

Nowhere are illusions about freedom more fostered than

in our educational system. When I think of my undergraduate college—Victoria College, University of Toronto—I think immediately of those huge words from the Bible carved in stone over the front door: "The truth shall make you free." [78] After spending ten years at three institutions of "higher learning" I have concluded that these words are irrelevant to the universities, since none of them knows anything about "the truth," nor indeed do they graduate "free" people. The university has become in our time a place for reinforcing the values, ideals, and abstractions of a progress-oriented, technological, ever-expanding economy— the aim being to produce graduates who will conform to these values and promote the ideology. In a society mindlessly devoted to consumerism, knowledge is packaged in convenient pieces and fed to youth with little regard to the interests and concerns of the student. I contend that this does not constitute education for freedom.

In this connection it is worth considering the social situation of a couple of millennia ago in ancient China.[79] In those times life was lived according to the tenets of Confucianism, which is more like an ethical system than a religion as we understand it. The commonsense formulas of this philosophy aimed at providing a stable social order by promoting virtuous and ordered action in the household, society, and government. Confuciansm was, in short, founded upon the abstract systems of language and law, ethical principles, and ritual behavior, and was therefore a system that promoted the order and conformity required for a settled society.

Now every social system breeds rebels, and the ancient Chinese rebel was the Taoist, who was typically an older person beyond the cares of the family and community. The Taoist rebels tended to retire from active community life, forming hermit communities in the hills. The Taoist hermits could be regarded as "subversives" in the sense that they systematically undermined the conventional assumptions of the Confucian order.

They accomplished this by questioning all ideas *about* life and all traditional ways of *seeing* life, urging instead a direct plunge into it. They further questioned such "progressive" social conventions as the idea that there can be an All-Good society, *yang* without *yin*, White without Black, Truth without Deception, Friends without Enemies. And finally they taught the contradictions inherent in "action" or "doing" (*wei*), and the value therefore in "acting without action," "doing without doing" (*wei wu wei*), or in positive terms doing things "naturally" or "spontaneously" (*tzu-jan*). In contrast to the forced action of governmental power, the Taoist cultivated the art of moving with nature, bending with the wind, the "gentle art" (*judo*) of "fading" from the blows rather than confronting them head on. The whole process was one of reeducating oneself to act directly or instinctively rather than thinking about action, or worse, thinking about thought.

The Taoist philosophy was designed to free people from conventional grids, traditional ideas, progressive ideologies, and the rigid laws of the ordered society. The Taoists realized that hanging on to permanent ideas and traditional dogmas is a tiring business and completely opposed to the un-self-consciousness of nature itself—including children in their "natural" state before they are taught to conform to conventional rules.

What we appear to lack in modern society is an equivalent of the Taoist rebel. Since the absolutes of religion have always aligned themselves with the conventions of community behavior, the total rebel has always lacked any alternative authority for his rebellion. This has remained the case even today, when church authority has been passed over to the certification procedures of the universities. Here authorities and conventions are connected to governmental funding and public donations, so that the university can merely cater to societal convention.

What passes for "rebellion" in Western society has never achieved the radical examination of fundamental assumptions achieved in ancient Chinese Taoism. A rebel today merely puts forth new "goals" or alternative ideological methods without ever questioning the assumption of "progress" he shares with the goals he rejects. Moreover, most rebels get caught in the trap of trying to be "original" —which simply assumes the same ego-centric identity of the society they reject. If, now and then, a really rebellious thinker emerges, he is in danger of being without a "position" and without a publisher!

But since the university now stands more at the crossroads than any religious or political institution, and since the university seems to enjoy undaunted prestige among the people—even despite its almost total subversion of religious and moral principles—it might profitably become the focal point for a program of education for *freedom*. As such, its task would be to expose students to ideas and culture in the grand tradition of Cardinal Newman[80] and Matthew Arnold [81]—*not* so that the student will eventually find a "true" idea to which he can then become enslaved, but so that he can eventually be free enough to "see through" all ideas.

This is an admittedly subversive way of looking at education. But witness the alternatives. The present university faculties are so adamant in presenting ideas, ideas, and more ideas with fervor that most students suspect the whole academic community of being on a perpetual and irrelevant head-trip. Indeed, the really "big name" faculty member is precisely that scholar who has powerful and persuasive ideas, usually containing their own self-verification principle—as does Biblical fundamentalism. These he bulldozes into overcrowded courses full of a captive audience of students with the ruthless logic of an election campaign or a hellfire sermon. Eventually students rebel against this Apollonian approach to things, suspecting that life may have more to it than ideas from the Great Books.

A few students react in the predictable way, by abandoning thinking of any sort and becoming completely Dionysian, going wild with undisciplined pranks in the dorms, sex in the pot, grass in the woods, an orgiastic spate of one lost weekend after another—believing that such sensual indulgence proves they are "free" from the rules of parents and professors. Eventually they graduate and slip into the docile consumerism of their parent society.

The other tendency is represented by innumerable student "radicals" who rebel against their professors' ideas by adopting different ones. Thus we find a core of protesters and picketers on every major university campus who appear wherever they can find a tinge of "racism," "liberalism," or the "exploitation" of workers—most of which comes out as "fascism"! Shouting their own ruthless logic of "Revolution!" they pretend to be free because they read Marx or Lenin or Stalin or Mao rather than Freud or Keynes or Galbraith! In the process of asserting this freedom, such radical types get so locked into their "revolutionary" ideals, Marxist dialectics, and Mao-think, so convinced that what they think is the absolute, rational Truth, that they become more Apollonian than their liberal professors.

The truth does not make men free when the "truth" is

seen as the supremacy of one theory above the rest, or when it compels behavior toward predetermined goals. But this is part of the hidden curriculum carried out of the lecture hall by students rebelling against American ideals and ideology. It is no accident, then, that interdepartmental rivalry, inner-departmental competition, and the occasional fierce debate between scholars in the journals over trivia are echoed within the radical cliques, where student leaders wrangle for hours over their various theories of how The Revolution ought to be run! In both cases human beings have become as enslaved by their ideas and abstractions as the Birchers, the Fundamentalists, or the Defense Department.

Freedom in the university means freedom from the tyranny of words and ideas, release from the radical rhetoric of ideologies that can only lead directly into confrontation, conflict, and violence—and thereafter to its immediate result: law and order, suppression and oppression.

What we need in the university is a department dedicated to the intellectual equivalent of "fragging"—which refers to the act of "fragmenting" a superior military officer with a well-placed grenade. This procedure occurs when officers continually send their men into dangerous situations, such as routing out the enemy in thick jungles rigged and bugged and mined by the enemy. Intellectual fragging is a process of education designed as a defense against *dangerous* ideas, meaning any idea constricting or imprisoning the mind rather than opening it up. Educational fragging is a technique of "subversive" learning, which is unfortunately only hinted at in *Teaching as a Subversive Activity*.[82] It is aimed at questioning, breaking up, and exposing the fundamental assumptions of all conventional ideas—until the student realizes how fragile, uncertain, restricting, and relative all such ideas are.

This process begins at the sensory level, so that the student discovers how color and sound and texture are "put on" the world by his senses, in the same way that a third dimension is put onto a two-dimensional photograph by the mind. Educational fragging then moves to language itself, exposing how our words divide the universe into the "in here" and the "out there," the good and the bad, order and chaos, pleasure and pain, space and solid. From here the ground is laid for a critique of the whole organism/environment split, including the fragmentation of society into "us" and "them," ourselves and our enemies.

The student is eventually led into the incredible contradictions and knots that result when the organism isolates itself and then proceeds to "conquer" its surroundings. The whole social pasteboard of roles and masks is gradually stripped away as the student learns that all his habits, ideas, beliefs, creeds, and absolutes are false securities against a universe that is fundamentally slippery. He begins to see that his entire culture—virtually every piece of literature since *The Book of Job* and *The Odyssey*—is plotted on the assumption that man is best understood as an ego. Gradually he understands how his own ego is reinforced by advertising, by movies, television programming, and the comics. He begins to see how his interaction is basically limited to ego-games—including even his "liberated" stance that he is not playing an ego-game! Eventually he comes to see the difference between symbols and the reality they represent, between real needs and the abstract "needs" of a consumer society, between the "wisdom of insecurity" [83] and the foolishness of paper "securities," between money and real wealth, between a Playmate and a woman.

Eventually the student is led into questions of Time, History, and Progress associated with philosophies, theologies, and political ideologies. He learns to see that relativity means that no one knows what is truly "basic," truly "profound," or when we are really moving "ahead." He learns that a universe with no bottom allows no sure footing. He discovers that a cosmos constructed as a laminated web of interaction does not allow complete "control" or "predictability." He discovers that deciding on any kind of action for a given purpose is impossible, since no action works in isolation. He begins to understand that solving the mystery of DNA, or inventing self-programming computers, or exploring the planets is only superficially understood as "progress." He discovers that there are no "higher" principles or "basic" laws on which to build a perfect civilization.

What he discovers, in short, is that his universe is not completely consistent. He discovers that the Final, True, Unified Everything Theory of How Things Are will have to include either a Random Loop or a Surprise Button, just as the original heaven included a skulking traitor with the improbable name of Luci-fer, The Light-Bearer! For the universe keeps throwing out psychic freaks and cripples, mongolians, geniuses, dwarfs, six-toed cats, and nectarines. Eventually the student discovers the profoundly simple truth that if there were only one way for things to be done, then obviously everything would be done that way!

The duration of this fragging process would be the full four years of undergraduate education and would culminate in a seminar called The Senior Frag. The purpose of the Senior Frag would not be to finalize a point of view but to reinforce uncertainty about every point of view. This seminar would therefore put to practice the non-wisdom gleaned from being free of ideas and abstractions. It would include a year-long communal encounter aimed at direct experience and the development of feeling. It would include sense exploration and mental insearch, the examination and sharing of dreams, and the exploration of the imagination. As it progressed, it would take the form of an in-depth exploration of art and music, architecture and religion, cell structure, evolution, and astronomy—without the constraint of coming up with some kind of "result," "conclusion," or "mature view." Finally, the student could elect to graduate or not, thus demonstrating his degree of freedom from a paper-certificate economy.

Now this is an e-ducation—in the literal Latin sense of leading out: being led out of the webs and binds of words and theories that are spun around students in lecture after lecture, course after course, year after year.

There are, of course, occasional students who manage to obtain this kind of "fragging" on their own. Here is part of the preface to an essay written by a student of mine at Stanford University who had somehow managed to conduct his own educational fragging:

> I'm not sure, but I think you're similar to me because I think both of us are human beings. Have you ever asked questions like "Why am I?" "Why do you think there's 'good' and 'bad'?" "Why is man?" "Why do I ask these questions?" I think, but I'm not certain, that there is no one "correct" answer (if any) to these questions. I'm not even certain just what I mean by "I" (or "you," for that matter). I think, but I'm not certain, that I'm changing. I'm not certain just what I mean by "changing." I think, but I'm not certain, that certainty and consistency are conventions that "exist" only in my "mind," to make an arbitrary distinction that "exists" only in my mind. I'm not certain just what I mean by " 'exists' only in my 'mind.' " I'm not

certain, but I think I construct the distinctions I think I "find" between us. I am certain that it's easy to inadvertently tie myself into a knot.[84]

Accustomed as we are to people with very definite opinions, obvious prejudices, and entrenched beliefs, we are apt to regard this student as inept, incompetent, or nonfunctional. But there is a world of difference between philosophical uncertainty and competence in life. The student-writer of this is earning his way through university by running rafts on the Colorado River through the Grand Canyon.

Freedom, then, is the willingness to live with total uncertainty, accepting the fact that the world has no foundation and the universe no bottom, and that clinging to creeds, symbols, systems, abstractions, or absolutes is the dis-ease of the privatized ego. It is, however, almost impossible to know how "I" ought to stop being isolated, since "I" *am* exactly that feeling of isolation. To take this ego-isolation seriously enough to try to let go of it is to reinforce the isolation while concealing it under the pretension of not taking it seriously. What this amounts to is a problem given to me with the warning that any thinking about it is guaranteed to produce the wrong answer.

Tied to thinking as I am, and not knowing quite how to solve a problem that requires no thought, I begin to feel myself in a hopeless muddle. The problem of being free begins to look something like the problem of developing a convincing proof that all circles are squares. Tackling such a problem inevitably means that every step in the logic will look ridiculous.

The fact is that I simply cannot discover how to acquire

freedom, since my enslavement is precisely such efforts at acquisition. Perhaps, then, I need to put forth an effortless effort or inactive action—but this seems quite impossible. I cannot put forth effort effortlessly, nor can I be inactively active. Indeed, the whole endeavor is like being told you must look at something, say a very beautiful woman, without seeing her!

We often look at people without seeing them, but if we try to do so, we find it cannot be done. Trying to look without seeing, to listen without hearing, or to touch without feeling is therefore a double bind in which two orders frustrate each other, like a thermostat that is set so precisely as to maintain a temperature of *exactly* 72 degrees. If the switch is "on," the arrival of a temperature of 72 degrees will mean "off," whereas if the switch is "off," the arrival of a temperature of 72 degrees will mean "on." The whole decision-making process quickly breaks down, which is why a double bind produces a feeling of paralysis. You must but you can't.

It seems obvious, then, that since I cannot help seeing a beautiful woman when I look at her or hearing her voice when I listen to it, my seeing and hearing is unintentional, spontaneous, and out of "my" control. In the same way, if I cannot help being enslaved to my ego and its ideas when I pursue freedom, then my ego-enslavement is out of "my" control. This is to say that even the so-called deliberate acts of my ego arise undeliberately from the much broader organism/environment field.

Suddenly the whole idea that I can be enslaved to my ego, my intellect, and my rational intentions collapses. I realize that my intentions are unintended, my acts are undeliberated, and my efforts are neither "mine" nor much of an "effort" at all. I realize that I cannot avoid being free, since even my *feeling* of conscious enslavement arises freely from the unconscious.

Once I feel this, I can suddenly see through everything. I understand and feel that I am free and always have been. Even the most apparently constricting poses that "I" assume are not "mine" but are freely adopted by the Universe-at-Large. I discover that all the devious ideas, ideals and ideologies, plans, programs, systems, symbols, abstractions, and absolutes are still here, but they no longer enslave me. Being free of them, I find I can adopt at will a Marxist pose or a capitalist one, a conservative position or a radical one, without staking my life on their truth. I can argue the merits of Christian mythology or secular atheism, Hinduism or Judaism, law and order or *laissez-faire,* mentalism or materialism, behaviorism or psychoanalysis—without feeling that any of these "positions" requires consistent commitment. In short, I find myself free to think without being enslaved to my thoughts.

This freedom, then, spells an end to "commitment," particularly that kind glorified by religious sects, revolutionary groups, national governments, and most social institutions. For this sort of commitment means precisely that enslavement to dogmas and ideologies which has led to religious wars in the past and nationalistic wars today. Founded upon the pattern of "My country right or wrong!" commitment is a sophisticated rationalization for the rational ego to cling to "the truth" it has found without the inconvenience of a further search. Such is the laziness that spells out the doom of humanity in our time.

If there is a commitment worth the name, it is commitment to the adventure and uncertainties of life itself—the daring that has led to such a far-out enterprise as human beings playing games on a planet somewhere in a slow-turning galaxy. But this is not a commitment that "we" have made, but rather one the whole universe embarked upon a long time ago.

Felt this way, the world seems to have a strange togetherness about It-All. The apparent division between the In-Here and the Out-There does not cease to exist. It simply ceases to be a problem, in the same way that the difference between mountains and valleys is no problem. Mountains and valleys become problematic only if we insist that there be nothing but mountains or nothing but valleys. In either case the world becomes uniformly flat, the only difference being the "elevation" of the flatness.

In the same way, the tremendous variety of opinion ceases to be a problem, and the insistence that we ought to get everybody together on every issue is seen as pure nonsense. The world becomes a delight—even the world of fanatical ideas—precisely because it is moving, living, and dynamic without ever settling down to a stable pattern.

Finally I realize that my aim is not to get everybody hitched up to the only freedom. What a bore that would be! For when I begin to "fantasize" about IT—about the Ultimate, Nameless Reality which men in former times called God—I realize that *this* world, *this* universe, *this* very tangle of ideological enslavement is precisely the world *I* would have made if I had done it myself.

For if I were God, if I were the Whole Universe, *if I were* IT (What a responsibility!)—I would immediately start trying to "get out of IT" as much as possible. This is to say that if, in the beginning, way back before there was any time, there was only IT, then IT must have been very lonely and very helpless, since IT was both everything and nothing. There would have been, in fact, no way to tell IT from pure emptiness. IT was obviously a very frustrating business.

But on the other hand, to *really* "get out of IT," IT would have to have started this way, as a black and empty void, a Wholly Holy Hole beyond all things but out of which "all things" could come, like spokes from an empty hub. Beginning this way, as Empty Nothingness, IT would obviously "start something" by livening things up with a game.

Now of course a game means that someone has to be It, and since there was no one else to be It, IT was It. But IT had also to hide IT-Self, since there was obviously no one else to hide. So IT went and hid, and IT went out to seek IT-self hiding from IT-Self. The end result of this rather far-out game was that IT ceased to be IT and went into hiding as everything else.

The whole point of this game is, of course, not to let IT get dull. Thus, to make the whole game worth the candle, IT rises and falls in mountains and valleys, comes and goes in dawn and dusk, lives and dies in orchids and elephants, and waxes and wanes in the moon. Sometimes IT is almost nothing, but at other times there is a lot to IT, as when IT finally becomes a really Big Star. The point is, however, that IT is hiding everywhere, even in those places where you would least expect IT.

Now this little story is precisely that innermost truth about things as understood by the ancient Hindus. According to Hindu mythology, Brahman (IT: the Godhead) hides as the *atman* (Self) of every man. This is called the *lila* of Brahman, which means his play, sport, pastime, diversion, or amusement. This myth forms one of the central themes in the Hindu *Chhandogya Upanishad—tat tvam asi,* or "That art Thou." In more contemporary terms, YOU are IT!

Since IT is hiding from IT-self, IT turns out to be YOU —only you probably don't know IT. Indeed, you probably go around looking for IT, not knowing that IT is doing the looking—just as you go about looking for freedom, not knowing that you are freely looking! Weird.

Does IT matter? Of course: IT "matters" all over the place, which is to say IT "birds" and "trees" and "peoples." IT is a big dance, a cosmic frug, a continual rhythm of hide/seek, lost/found, now-you-see-IT/now-you-don't. Anyone who cannot see IT "itting" IT all over the place cannot see anything, for everything is IT.

What's IT all about? IT is all about everything, since IT is anything you can name. IT is up to anything and everything. Doing your own thing is doing virtually anything, since everything is where IT's at. But you can never really under-stand what IT's all about, for IT is standing-under you. You can get in a terrible mess if you forget that you doing IT is really IT doing you. The biggest mistake, then, is to try to over-do or out-do IT, rather than simply getting *with* IT. Nor is getting with IT difficult, since you are where IT's at, and that doesn't have to be anyplace special.

Does IT make a difference? Of course: IT makes all the differences. That's ITS game—always hiding differently from the last time. Thus IT does the people-game differently since (Remember!) IT is trying to hide from IT-self. Unless IT does it differently, IT all becomes a terrible bore. Hiding from IT is largely a matter of finding ever-new hiding places. Thus every time IT "peoples," a brand-new hiding-place-baby is born. IT is very clever at hiding—as you will notice if you look around at IT all.

Can you avoid IT? Hardly, since YOU are IT. Can you

avoid the Avoider? In the same way, you can never fully know IT because IT always does the knowing. Like a mirror trying to reflect itself, you are soon bewildered and bedazzled if you try.

But what, then, is the point of IT? Precisely: IT has no point, or, rather, IT is all points. There is no point and no place where IT isn't. IT rains and IT snows and sometimes IT is cloudy, sometimes bright. IT is into everything and is therefore absolutely central to everything that happens. Even at death IT is right in there, getting ready to do you over. And once you die, IT does what IT has always done. IT hides IT-Self so that IT can "I" IT-self again. And thus "I" will be undone and done again—by IT.

Now I predict that there will be someone out there who will not accept IT. Predictably, he will be a sophisticated man of the world busy with his business, insecure with his securities, obsessed with his possessions. Not realizing that he is IT, he thinks instead that he is an intelligent ego trapped in a stupid universe. But the trapped ego is simply one of the very best hiding places IT ever devised—a place so scary, so terrible, so absolutely vulnerable that the whole galaxy seems to be piled upon ITS head, so frustrating that IT cries out in agony that IT is all completely meaningless! This poor little ragamuffin ego goes about looking for IT and asking about IT, or else gives IT all up and commits suicide—which is a really scary and daring thing for IT to do.

Everyone is, of course, free to do IT his own way, even if that means being completely enslaved to ideas about IT rather than simply experiencing IT. Some will go searching for IT, and that's what *gurus* are for. But too much searching is calculated to miss IT, and every good *guru* knows this. Every time a new student appears, the good *guru* laughs to himself and thinks, "Here IT comes again." That's why he has that funny look in his eyes. But then if you go looking for IT, not feeling that you are IT doing the looking and feeling, you deserve to be laughed at. That is why laughter is always where IT's at.

And so, when IT comes right down to IT, IT is the Joker in the deck. But since everything is IT, the whole deck is a joke. So now you know why all the angels in Dante's Heaven are laughing fit to kill. They're laughing at you and with you, though you don't know it. They're laughing *at* you because you don't know IT. They're laughing *with* YOU because YOU are IT, and so are they. So there you have IT. At last you are free to laugh at IT too.

Notes

1. R. D. Laing, *Knots* (Pantheon Books, Inc., 1970).
2. Julian Huxley, *Religion Without Revelation* (New American Library, Inc., Mentor Books, 1959), p. 59.
3. William A. Clebsch, *From Sacred to Profane America: The Role of Religion in American History* (Harper & Row, Publishers, Inc., 1968), pp. 17, 19, 207-218.
4. Winston Churchill, quoted in Adrienne Koch (ed.), *Philosophy for a Time of Crisis* (E. P. Dutton & Company, Inc., 1959), pp. 21-22.
5. Wing-tsit Chan (ed. and tr.), *The Way of Lao Tzu* (The Bobbs-Merrill Company, Inc., 1963), no. 57.
6. Lin Yutang (ed. and tr.), *The Wisdom of Confucius* (Random House, Inc., 1938), p. 137.
7. John K. Ryan (tr.), *The Confessions of St. Augustine* (Doubleday & Company, Inc., Image Books, 1960), Bk. VIII, Ch. 7, p. 194.
8. For an excellent discussion of the "irrigation city," see Peter Drucker, "The First Technological Revolution and Its Lesson," *Technology, Management and Society* (Harper & Brothers, 1958), pp. 117-128. "Hydraulic civilization" is Karl A. Wittvogel's phrase for which see "The Hydraulic Civilizations," *Man's Role in Changing the Face of the Earth*, ed. by William L. Thomas, Jr. (The University of Chicago Press, 1956), pp. 152-164.

9. Ryan, *op. cit.*, Bk. XI, Ch. 14, p. 287.

10. Oswald Spengler, *The Decline of the West,* abr. by Helmut Werner (Alfred A. Knopf, Inc., 1962), pp. 7-11.

11. For a fascinating excursion into the mystical "here and now" of Christian mythology, see Alan W. Watts, *Myth and Ritual in Christianity* (London: Thames & Hudson, Ltd., 1954), a book for which there is no substitute.

12. Ananda K. Coomaraswamy, *Hinduism and Buddhism* (Philosophical Library, Inc., 1943), p. 33, n. 21.

13. B. F. Skinner's *Beyond Freedom and Dignity* (Alfred A. Knopf, Inc., 1971) is the lastest restatement of ideas about social devolpment and cultural design through behavioral control which Skinner worked out in fictional form in *Walden Two* (The Macmillan Company, 1948).

14. John Platt, *Perception and Change: Projections for Survival* (University of Michigan Press, 1970), p. 160.

15. Alvin Toffler, *Future Shock* (Random House, Inc., 1970).

16. A. H. Chapman, *The Strategy of Sex* (G. P. Putnam's Sons, 1969).

17. Eric Berne, *Games People Play: The Psychology of Human Relationships* (Grove Press, Inc., 1964). For a much broader application of game-theory to culture, see Johan Huizinga, *Homo Ludens: A Study of the Play Element in Culture* (Beacon Press, Inc., 1955).

18. Trigant Burrow, *The Neurosis of Man: An Introduction to a Science of Human Behavior* (London: Routledge & Kegan Paul, Ltd., 1949), pp. 4-5.

19. R. D. Laing, *The Politics of Experience* (Ballantine Books, Inc., 1968), p. 46.

20. Skinner, *Beyond Freedom and Dignity,* p. 199.

21. Alexander Lowen, "In Defense of Modesty," *The Journal of Sex Research,* Vol. IV, No. 1 (Feb., 1968), p. 52.

22. Julian Huxley, in *Perspectives in Biology and Medicine,* Vol. VIII, No. 4 (1964), p. 410.

23. Esther and William Menaker, *Ego in Evolution* (Grove Press, Inc., 1965), p. 13.

24. Robert S. De Ropp, *The Master Game: Pathways to Higher Consciousness Beyond the Drug Experience* (Delta Books, 1969), pp. 93-108.

25. Laing, *The Politics of Experience*, p. 55.

26. Skinner, *Beyond Freedom and Dignity,* especially Ch. 1.

27. Alan Watts, *Does It Matter? Essays on Man's Relation to Materiality* (Pantheon Books, Inc., 1970), p. 25.

28. Alan Watts, *The Way of Zen* (Pantheon Books, Inc., 1957), pp. 126, 127.

29. Victor White, *God and the Unconscious* (London: The Harvill Press, Ltd., 1952), p. 25.

30. "Axial period" is Karl Jaspers' term. For an extensive though highly generalized discussion, see Lewis Mumford, "Axial Man," *The Transformations of Man* (Collier Books, 1962), pp. 59-81.

31. Chan, *op. cit.*, nos. 2 and 22.

32. *Ibid.*, nos. 1 and 4.

33. I Cor. 1:25 (RSV).

34. I Cor. 2:10 (NEB).

35. Alan Watts, *Nature, Man and Woman* (Pantheon Books, Inc., 1958), p. 34.

36. C. G. Jung, *Memories, Dreams, Reflections* (Pantheon Books, Inc., 1961), p. 302.

37. Theodore Roszak, *The Making of a Counter Culture: Reflections on the Technocratic Society and Its Youthful Opposition* (Doubleday & Company, Inc., Anchor Books, 1969), pp. 205-238.

38. J. Krishnamurti, *Freedom from the Known* (Harper & Row, Publishers, Inc., 1969).

39. William James, *Essays in Radical Empiricism and A Pluralistic Universe* (E. P. Dutton & Company, Inc., 1971), p. 143.

40. Chan, *op. cit.*, no. 56.

41. Burton Watson (tr.), *Chuang Tzu: Basic Writings* (Columbia University Press, 1964), pp. 39-40.

42. See Anton C. Pegis (ed.), *Basic Writings of Saint Thomas Aquinas,* 2 vols. (Random House, Inc., 1945), Vol. I, QQ. 3, 7, 9-11.

43. See, for example, A. C. Bouquet, *The Christian Faith and Non-Christian Religions* (London: James Nisbet & Co., Ltd., 1958), or his earlier *Comparative Religion* (Hammondsworth, Middlesex: Penguin Books, Ltd., 1941); Herbert H. Farmer, *Revelation and Religion* (Harper & Brothers, 1954); and Hendrik Kraemer, *The Christian Message in a Non-Christian World* (Harper & Brothers, 1938).

44. Buckminster Fuller, *No More Secondhand God and Other Writings* (Southern Illinois University Press, 1963), p. 35.

45. *Playboy,* Vol. XVIII, No. 7 (July, 1971), pp. 103-104.

46. T. S. Eliot, "The Waste Land."

47. Bertrand Russell, *Why I Am Not a Christian* (Simon and Schuster, Inc., 1957), p. 107.

48. Dylan Thomas, "Do Not Go Gentle Into That Good Night."

49. See John Wilson, "Film Literacy in Africa," *Canadian Communications,* Vol. I, No. 4 (Summer, 1961), pp. 7-14.

50. See Charles A. Reich, *The Greening of America* (Random House, Inc., 1970), pp. 87-156.

51. Henry David Thoreau, "Civil Disobedience," in Carl Bode (ed.), *The Portable Thoreau* (The Viking Press, Inc., 1947), p. 126.

52. Alfred North Whitehead, *Modes of Thought* (Capricorn Books, G. P. Putnam's Sons, 1958), pp. 197, 202-232.

53. Pierre Teilhard de Chardin, *Man's Place in Nature* (London: William Collins Sons & Co., Ltd., 1966), p. 18.

54. Pierre Teilhard de Chardin, *The Phenomenon of Man* (London: William Collins Sons & Co., Ltd., 1959), pp. 53-66.

55. Lewis Carroll, *Through the Looking-Glass and What Alice Found There,* Ch. 1.

56. Nicolas Berdyaev, quoted in Stuart Chase, *The Tyranny*

of Words (Harcourt, Brace and World, Inc., A Harvest Book, 1938), pp. 99-100.

57. Alfred North Whitehead, *Science and the Modern World* (The Free Press, 1967), p. 51.

58. Chase, *op. cit.,* p. 91.

59. Ryan, *op. cit.,* Bk. XI, Ch. 12, p. 286.

60. With thanks to Richard Schwartz.

61. One of the best psychological discussions of demons and monsters is to be found in Alexander Lowen, *The Betrayal of the Body* (The Macmillan Company, Collier Books, 1969), pp. 128-144.

62. Bernard Gunther, *Sense Relaxation: Below Your Mind* (The Macmillan Company, Collier Books, 1968), p. 59.

63. Laing, *Politics of Experience,* p. 75.

64. *Ibid.,* p. 81.

65. *Ibid.,* pp. 83-84.

66. Reich, *op. cit.,* p. 107.

67. L. Charles Birch, *Nature and God* (London: SCM Press, Ltd., 1965), p. 95.

68. Alexander Lowen, *The Language of the Body* (The Macmillan Company, Collier Books, 1971), pp. 134-135.

69. See *Science,* Vol. CXXXIX (1963), pp. 884-890.

70. Ernest Hemingway, quoted in Neil Postman and Charles Weingartner, *Teaching as a Subversive Activity* (Delacorte Press Book, 1969), p. 3.

71. Victor Zuckerkandl, *Sound and Symbol: Music and the External World* (Princeton University Press, 1969), p. 260.

72. Peter Madison, "Coming of Age at College," *Psychology Today,* Vol. V, No. 5 (October, 1971).

73. James Hillman, *Insearch: Psychology and Religion* (Charles Scribner's Sons, 1967), pp. 72-73.

74. Most well known is the Indian god Shiva—as Nataraja, Lord of the Dance—usually depicted as dancing on a dwarfish demon called Apasmara Purusha, the "Demon of Forgetfulness." This is paralleled by Japanese statues of Tobatsu Bishamon Ten, Guardian of the North Quarter of the Buddhist heaven.

Typical is the one in the Buddhist Temple Kanzeon-ji in Fuku-oka, seen standing upon the palms of Jiten, God of Earth, accompanied by two goblins. A quite opposite tradition with which we are most familiar fails to see such monsters as *supporting* the rational side of life. Found in both the East and the West, the relationship between gods and monsters is turned into violent conflict: Indra slaying the monster Vritra; Marduk slaying Tiamat; God banishing Satan from heaven.

75. John Kenneth Galbraith, "Who Minds the Store?" *The New York Times,* October 26, 1970, p. 35.

76. Chan, *op. cit.,* no. 4.

77. See David T. Bazelon, *The Paper Economy* (Random House, Inc., Vintage Books, 1959); also Alan Watts, "Wealth Versus Money," *Does It Matter?,* pp. 3-24.

78. John 8:32 (KJV).

79. See Watts, *The Way of Zen,* Ch. 1, especially pp. 10 ff.

80. John Henry Newman, *On the Scope and Nature of University Education,* delivered as a series of eight discourses in 1852 at the founding of the Irish Catholic University at Dublin. This work still stands as one of the keystones of literature on "liberal education," particularly Discourses IV-VII.

81. Matthew Arnold's *Culture and Anarchy* (1869) is one of the more important tracts in the history of *education,* which is disguised under the nineteenth-century rubric of "culture."

82. Postman and Weingartner, *op. cit.*

83. Alan Watts's *The Wisdom of Insecurity* (Pantheon Books, Inc., 1951) not only carries through many of the themes in the present work but is also the best introductory work for the beginning reader of the many works of this fascinating writer.

84. With thanks to Peter Winn for permission to quote from his essay "Crucifying Privacy."

About the Author

BARRY WOOD is a Canadian, who holds a B.A. from the University of Toronto and an M.A. from the University of British Columbia. THE ONLY FREEDOM is his second book and was written while he was a student at Stanford University during the completion of an interdisciplinary doctoral program in English and American Literature, Humanities, and Religious Studies. He has taught high school, worked as a computer programmer, and since entering graduate school, has held teaching assistantships in English, Advanced Writing, World Literature and the History of Ideas, and Religious Philosophy.

In 1970 his book *The Magnificent Frolic* was published. Overturning many traditional ideas about religion, this revolutionary book offered a new option for contemporary minds. Drawing on a linguistic theory developed by Benjamin Lee Whorf, Barry Wood developed what he now calls a "religion of experience." John A. T. Robinson described it as "a highly creative way through and beyond the 'death of God,' when many, including myself, have been wondering whether perhaps this was not a dead end. An exhilarating book."

Since the publication of *The Magnificent Frolic*, Barry

Wood has conducted a number of talks and seminars on religion, ecology, and freedom with various college and church groups. His approach is always to lay bare fundamental assumptions, to make difficult ideas as accessible as possible, and to integrate knowledge with experience. His contributions to *The Stanford Daily* have included numerous editorials on ecology and education, and reviews of books and contemporary music.

Throughout his four years as a graduate student at Stanford, Barry Wood held a Doctoral Fellowship from The Canada Council. He has recently moved to the University of Houston, where he now teaches literature in the Department of English.